TABLE OF CONTENTS

INTRODUCTION

Background

In a speech to the American Enterprise Institute in late February 2003, President George Bush compared the problems faced in the creation of democratic societies in Germany and Japan to those in Iraq and Afghanistan. During his thirty-minute speech, the President mentioned the words "Germany" and "Japan" once each. His brief mention of the two countries, made in the greater context of nation building, quickly ignited debate into the validity of his comparison.[1] Pundits, generally divided along political party lines, rushed to the sound of battle, introducing evidence such as economic factors, predilection toward democracy, diligent workforce, and infrastructure to support their arguments. Experts offered mixed opinions to the comparison. Dr. James Dobbins, leader of a team of RAND researchers that studied nation building efforts of the United States in seven historical cases stated, "the cases of Germany and Japan set a standard for postconflict nation-building that has not been matched since. Both were comprehensive efforts at social, political, and economic reconstruction."[2] Other expert opinions seemed to change as time progressed. In a March 2003 interview with the *New York Times*, Pulitzer Prize winning author and historian Dr. John Dower stated, "I think there are both positive and negative lessons to be learned. The first challenge to be addressed is to alleviate the humanitarian crisis in an immediate, massive way. Then you have to give immediate attention to creating institutional structure for

---

[1]George Bush., *President Discusses the Future of Iraq*. Speech to the American Enterprise Institute, 26 February, 2003. Online at http://www.whitehouse.gov/news/releases/2003/ 02/ 20030226-11 html.
    [2] James Dobbins. "Nation Building: The Inescapable Responsibility of the World's Only Superpower." *Rand Review*, Vol. 27, No. 2 (Summer 2003). Online at http://www rand.org/publications/ randreview/issues/summer2003/nation1 html. Accessed 18 January, 2003.

democracy. And you must mobilize popular support."[3] At the end of June, his tone began to change. "Looking back at occupied Japan should really remind us both how fundamentally different Iraq is from the Japan of 1945 and also how far the United States itself has departed from the ideals of a half-century ago."[4] By December, in an interview with the *Los Angeles Times*, he concluded, "The truth is that what is happening in Iraq presents a stunning and fundamental contrast to what took place in occupied Japan and Germany over half a century ago — and not a positive one."[5] Whether expert or pundit, most writers only considered the surface of the problem, failing to consider that there might be something deeper causing discontent that could prevent reconstruction. The omission may be because the President's speech focused only on the reconstruction of both nations—that is, the physical rebuilding of infrastructure and return of the nation to self-rule. What was missing was an acknowledgment of the necessity to change the ideological perspective of the populations of the two nations to permit reconstruction.

Although nationbuilding is a necessary and perhaps admirable intent, the deeper problem lies in the perceptions of an ideologically indoctrinated group of people toward the focus of their hatred. To simply apply the bandage of what Western society perceives as modern necessity ignores the impact of the true believers within the society. Their influence sours the process of nationbuilding by undermining the stability and security of the nation. A search for a historical example of a successful attempt to combat the ideologues and change the perspective of a nation leads one to post World War II Germany and Japan.

---

[3] John Dower. "Occupation Preoccupation," *New York Times,* March 30, 2003. Online at http://www.nytimes.com/2003/03/30/magazine/30QUESTIONS.html?ex=1074574800&en=635ca77f06e4 ba48&ei=5070. Accessed 18 January, 2004.

[4] John Dower. "Is the U.S. Repeating the Mistakes of Japan in the 1930s?." *History News Network*, June 30, 2003. Online at http://hnn.us/articles/1534 html Accessed 18 January 2004.

[5] John Dower. "Bush's Comparison of Iraq with Postwar Japan Ignores the Facts." *Los Angeles Times*, December 8, 2003.

Both Germany and Japan had populations that were indoctrinated into a totalitarian ideology defined by the state.[6] The Japanese Emperor possessed (in theory) complete control of all his subjects and was worshipped as a living god. It was inconceivable to the people of Japan that he could be wrong. Likewise, Adolf Hitler, though not worshipped as a god, was no less admired. His frenetic rants recalling the glory days of Germany inspired millions to actively join his cause. Defeat of the two leaders confused and disaffected millions of people in their respective societies, leaving a deep pool of potential adversaries ready to resist the efforts of the Allied nations. A similar dynamic can be observed today in the followers of Saddam Hussein, Osama Bin Laden, *al Qaeda*, and many of the fundamentalist Muslim faithful. Those under the spell of such modern day demagogues have repeatedly displayed their commitment to the doctrine of their masters by conducting suicide attacks against their enemies. Although there were no terrorist suicide attacks against Americans after World War II, the reconstructions of Japan and Germany were the last (and arguably only) successful attempts made by the United States to change the ideology of a population.

While successful, postwar Japan and Germany were neither the first nor the only international attempt to change the ideology of a nation or group of people. Leaders of Marxist/Leninist states such as the Soviet Union (USSR), China and North Korea imposed their values and social structure on the citizens of their countries. Of the three largest states, the Soviet Union has dissolved under its own weight, North Korea is unable to provide for its own people and China is moving away from its original Marxist doctrine toward a more free market economy. In addition to failure, the movements shared one main commonality. They were

---

[6] Edward Shils, "The Concept and Function of an Ideology." *International Encyclopedia of the Social Sciences. Volume 7.* (New York: The Macmillan Company and the Free Press, 1972) 66-76. Dr. Shills outlines nine areas that characterize an ideology and distinguish it from lesser movements. While the difference between and ideology and other activities such as outlooks, creeds, and beliefs is rarely more

attempts by larger countries (USSR and China) to use smaller countries (Warsaw Pact, North Korea and Vietnam) as shields for the homeland and as sources for economic gain.

Further removed in history, colonial powers such as Great Britain and France sought to impose their social order on their colonies with varying results. Though initially successful in some attempts, eventually almost all colonies were abandoned to their own devices. Again, the common thread in colonialism was territorial gain and economic exploitation for the greater good of the colonial nation.

Religion, combined with a belief in the ethnic and historical greatness of a group of people, has also played a significant part in attempts to change an ideology. History and current affairs are full of examples of forced, induced, and voluntary conversions of nations to varying religions. Missionaries worldwide have used methods ranging from simple teaching to wholesale slaughter of nonbelievers in their quest to spread the word of their religions. Dictators such as Saddam Hussein and Pol Pot have used the guise of religion and perceived historical greatness of their respective nations to leverage their legitimacy as they rise to power. Groups like *Al Quaeda* have infiltrated countries using religion as a counter to another undesirable force. Entire nations have used the patina of religion as an excuse to conquer others through war; usually for power, economic, or territorial profit.

Whether for gain of a single person, group of persons, nation, or religion, there has always been a tangible benefit in the form of money, power, afterlife, or immediate security for the ideological entity that conquerors another. What set Germany and Japan apart was that they were attempts to create a "better state of peace"[7] with little or no immediate return to the conquering nations except concord. In fact, in the immediate sense, the ventures cost the allies a

---

than a degree of application, both the Japanese situation and the rise of Nazism explicitly meet all nine features of an ideology.

significant amount in time, effort and money. The difference leads one to believe that Germany and Japan may offer valuable lessons learned from in the extremely difficult undertaking of defeating the ideology of a formerly totalitarian regime.

Readings on ideologies and mass movements give only sketchy insight as to how they might be defeated. In the early 1950s, Eric Hoffer stated,

> The vigor of a mass movement stems from the propensity of its followers for united action and self-sacrifice. When we ascribe the success of a movement to its faith, doctrine, propaganda, leadership, ruthlessness and so on, we are but referring to instruments of unification and to means used to inculcate a readiness for self-sacrifice.[8]

Three of Hoffer's considerations—faith, doctrine and leadership—can be argued to constitute the core unifying agents of a mass movement. All other unifying agents are simply in place to shore up the foundation. While not given strictly as a target for defeat of an ideology, it is one of the earliest uses (1951) of these three areas together as crucial to its maintenance.

More currently, Frederick D. Barton and Bathsheba N. Crocker of the Center for Strategic and International Studies describe the "Four Pillars of Reconstruction" as security, justice and reconciliation, social and economic well being, and governance and participation. Although education is not conspicuously integrated into the pillars, the descriptions for each pillar include an implicit requirement for education throughout the process.[9] The indoctrination of those involved makes it challenging to change their outlook. Despite the difficulty, many authorities agree that three areas must be considered when attacking an ideology—legitimacy,

---

[7] Basil H. Liddel-Hart, *Strategy* (New York: Signet, 1974) 353. Liddel Hart states, "The object of war is to create a better peace."
[8] Eric Hoffer. *The True Believer, Thoughts on the Nature of Mass Movements.* (New York: Harper and Row Eric Hoffer, 1951), 57
[9] Frederick D Barton, and Bathsheba N Crocker. "Post Conflict Reconstruction." (Washington, DC: Center for Strategic and International Studies) 2001. Online at http://www.csis.org/isp/pcr/framework.pdf.

reeducation, and economy.[10] But is there a deeper problem that must be addressed before legitimacy, reeducation, and economy can be tackled?

Delving deeper into the three core issues of an ideology, it becomes obvious that fear is an elemental component at the heart of the problem. Legitimacy of the government is driven by its ability to provide for the daily needs of its citizens—law and basic services—reducing fear of the present. Rebuilding of the economy, education about the new regime and return of people to work reduces fear of the future. Classroom education at all levels reduces fear for the next generation. If the three preconditions of legitimacy, economy and education are not met, each factor will build upon the others to increase the level of fear in a society until it becomes an overwhelming and unconquerable presence consuming every vestige of daily life. Overcoming fear that has so visibly manifested itself must therefore be the first task of any organization dedicated to defeating an ideology. Since the most prominent and proximate cause of fear is a lack of security in the present, establishment of security in daily life becomes the immediate requirement for defeat of an ideology. While the most tangible manifestation of a secure society is the return of law, it involves more than police on the street. The people of a society defined by fear have become numb to the possibility of change while their leaders have long since rationalized their crimes. A truly substantial embodiment of the return of law requires the

---

[10] Authoritative information can be found in readings on nationbuilding, insurgency and ideology. For further information see, Bard E. O'Neill *Insurgency & Terrorism: Inside Modern Revolutionary Warfare*. Washington DC: Brassey's Inc, 2001., Max G. Manwaring, "Toward an Understanding of Insurgency Wars: The Paradigm." In Max G. Manwaring, ed. *Uncomfortable Wars: Toward a New Paradigm of Low Intensity Conflict*. (Bolder, CO: Westview Press, 1991) Chapter 2. Mark Jurgensmeyer, *Terror in the Mind of God, The Global Rise of Religious Violence*. Berkeley: University of California Press, 2001., Bruce Hoffman, *Inside Terrorism*. New York: Columbia University Press, 1998., James Dobbins *et al. America's Role in Nation Building: From Germany to Iraq*. Santa Monica, CA: RAND,2003., Minxin Pei and Sara Kasper, "Lessons from the Past: The American Record in Nation-Building." Carnegie Endowment for International Peace. Online at http://www.ceip.org/files/pdf/ Policybrief24.pdf. [Accessed 2 March, 2004.] Internet., Ray Salvatore Jennings, "The Road Ahead: Lessons in Nation Building from Japan, Germany, and Afghanistan for Postwar Iraq," United States Institute of Peace Peaceworks #49 (7 May, 2003). Online at http://www.usip.org/pubs/peaceworks/ pwks49 html. Accessed 3 March, 2004, [Internet].

creation of a judicial organ to try and punish those the victor offers as guilty, creating a

perception of final justice and a break from the past. Since post World War II reconstruction, to

include the Nuremberg and Tokyo trials, have already been singled out as a possible example for

defeat of an ideology, the further question becomes evident. Do postwar Germany and Japan

provide lessons in the creation and implementation of a judicial system to try war criminals of the

former Iraqi regime?

Methodology

This monograph will begin with a brief overview of the planning for the occupation of

Germany and Japan. In the case of Germany, the focus will first be on the planning of Operations

RANKIN, TALISMAN, and ECLIPSE to show the depth of military planning that went into the

occupation, then on Combined Chiefs of Staff Directive Number 551 (CCS/551), and Joint Chiefs

of Staff Order Number 1067 (JCS 1067), highlighting the difficulties in political planning.[11] Case

studies in the planning for postwar Japan will paint a different picture. There, all efforts focused

on a purely military solution to war termination with little political planning or thought as to what

came after the conclusion of hostilities.

The first section will examine how the Allies arrived at the necessity to defeat the

legitimacy of the former leaders of Germany and Japan by means of war trials in both countries.

Beginning with a background and history of the Nuremberg and Tokyo trials we will analyze the

outcome and results. Next, we look at the legacy of the two trials and examine how they

influenced current international law. Following the discourse on international law, we will

---

[11]Operation RANKIN, the plan for post conflict operations in Europe initiated in May 1943. It was succeeded by operation TALISMAN, which was initiated after the successful Normandy landings and included a requirement for denazification. When TALISMAN was believed to be compromised, its name was changed to ECLIPSE with little change to the operational plan. The keystones of political planning were CCS/551 "Directive for the Military Government in Germany Prior to Defeat or Surrender" and JCS1067, the Morgenthau plan. All will be discussed in Chapter 2.

discuss the relevance of both trials to modern operations in Iraq, including possible application for current operations. The final chapter will contemplate the requirements for and results of a trial for the former leaders of Iraq in context of modern society.

Assumptions

This monograph is premised on three assumptions. First, the concept of nationbuilding is a recent (within the last century) idea that is devoid of any overt attempts at colonization, power grabs, economic gains or physical security for a homeland. It is characterized by the objective of building the internal structure of a stand-alone state for the sake of peace. The process is not intended to create an exploitable puppet of the nation that undertook the effort. Because of the enormous resources necessary in such an endeavor, few states in history (conceivably only the United States and USSR) have had the capability to attempt the process. Since the USSR overtly used the surrounding states of the Warsaw Pact as a security barrier and economic, military and social puppet of the Soviet state, none of its efforts meet the nationbuilding criteria. Therefore, only the United States, or any coalition / alliance that may form with the United States as a core, can be said to have attempted the process within the stated limits. Second, before a nationbuilding effort can begin in any formerly totalitarian regime with an ideological underpinning, there must be a plan to defeat the ideology. Third, the "denazification" of Germany and the reconstruction (or democratization) of Japan are the only successful instances in which the United States was able to change the ideology of a nation. As such, they can give insight into how one might defeat an ideology.

Limitations and Delimitations

This monograph is not intended to be a treatise on international law or its application with respect to the sociology and ideology of a region. Instead, it is an attempt to present a historic context in which to frame a trial for the former leaders of Iraq based upon lessons learned from the two seminal applications of international law: the Nuremberg Tribunal and Tokyo trials.

This monograph will examine the problem from three directions. The first focuses on eroding the legitimacy of the enemy leadership by employing war tribunals and trials. The second examines the evolution, current state, and requirements of international law and their impact on a trial in Iraq. Last will be the potential impact of the trials themselves. Although other areas may either propose differing ways to effect change in an ideologically based population or invite consideration into other directions from which to examine the problem, these three areas promise to be visible and easily implemented but simultaneously contentious and easily misunderstood. Despite the difficulty, the profit derived from proper execution is immense.

PLANNING THE PEACE

> Planning for termination of operations must be ongoing during
> all phases of COA development, deployment of forces, and
> execution of operations. [12]
> -Joint Publication 3.0, p. IV-20

Although the sheer magnitude of the Second World War would seem to have consumed

every person in and out of uniform with its daily grind, as the war moved inexorably toward

fruition, military and civilian leaders of the Allied nations expressed increasing concern over

what would come next. With the lessons of the "peace" after World War I fresh in their minds,

the Allied powers were loathe to make the same mistakes twice. As B. H. Liddell-Hart, a noted

British military theorist of the time, noted in *Strategy*, "If you concentrate exclusively on victory,

with no thought for the aftereffect, you may be too exhausted to profit by the peace, while it is

almost certain that the peace will be a bad one, containing the germs of another war." [13] With this

thought in mind, planning for the future of the defeated Axis nations would crescendo from a few

men with ideas into an all out blitz that rivaled the Normandy landings.

Military Planning

As early as 1942, the United States Army began to set up systems to ease the transfer to

postconflict operations with the creation of the Civil Affairs Training School at the University of

Chicago. [14] December 1943 saw the release of FM 27-5, *US Army and Navy Manual of Military

Government and Civil Affairs (OPNAV 50E-3)*. [15] Although well intended, the manual was clearly

focused on defeat of the Nazis in Europe. More detailed planning for postconflict operations in

---

[12] Joint Chiefs of Staff. *Doctrine for Joint Operations, Joint Publication 3-0.* Washington D.C.:
U.S. JCS, 10 September, 2001.
[13] Basil H. Liddel-Hart, *Strategy* (New York: Signet, 1974) 353.
[14] Lafe F. Allen, "Education Reform in Japan", The Yale Review, 36 (June 1947) 711.

Europe began in May, 1943 in the form of Operation RANKIN. With the Normandy invasion looming in the future, LTG Sir Frederick E. Morgan, Chief of Staff, Supreme Allied Commander (COSSAC) began planning for a sudden collapse of Germany. Although well intended, there was little direction for the planning staff to follow due to a lack of guidance from the highest levels of government toward postwar policy. Predictably, the plans for Operation RANKIN began lethargically. Determined to forge on with the planning process, Morgan produced a draft for the Quebec conference to be submitted to Prime Minister Churchill and President Roosevelt. The objective of the plan was, "to occupy, as rapidly as possible, appropriate areas from which we can take steps to enforce the terms of unconditional surrender…and in addition, to carry out the rehabilitation of the liberated countries." After a review of the order by the two leaders, Morgan was told to continue the planning effort. [16]

Following the successful Normandy landing, military leaders realized an increasing sense urgency toward the construction of a new plan for the occupation of Germany. The plan, code named TALISMAN, included a requirement for "denazification" of Germany. TALISMAN, which evolved into Operation ECLIPSE in October 1944, became the military plan for the occupation of Europe and military origin of the requirement for the "denazification" of Germany. [17]

Planning for Japan was much less organized. The intent to finish the war in Europe before concentrating on Pacific theater ensured the priority for planning and execution would be in the European theater until the defeat of the Nazis. The second place status of the Pacific

---

[15] War Department. *FM 27-5, US Army and Navy Manual of Military Government and Civil Affairs. (OPNAV 50E-3)* U.S. Government, 22 Dec 1943.
[16] McCreedy, Kenneth O. "Planning the Peace: Operation ECLIPSE and the Occupation of Germany," (Fort Leavenworth, Kans.: School for Advanced Military Studies, U.S. Army Command and General Staff College, 1995.)
[17] SHAEF. "Operation ECLIPSE, Appreciation and Outline Plan," Supreme HQ, Allied Expeditionary Force, 10 November 1944. (Hereafter cited as ECLPISE) This is noted in a memo dated 10

theater combined with the sheer hatred and lack of understanding of the Japanese culture created a blind spot in American planning. Accordingly, plans for Japan were limited to Operation OLYMPIC, the amphibious invasion of the southernmost island of Japan by thirteen divisions. OLYMPIC would be followed by CORONET, a twenty-three division thrust toward the economic heart of Japan: the Kanto Plain.[18] The two plans were essentially an attempt to defeat the Japanese through brute force. Upon completion, there would be enough Americans in country to do something, (at the time, undefined) with the people of Japan.

Once it was clear that the invasion would not be necessary, General Douglas MacArthur directed the planning of Project BLACKLIST, which would establish a military government through the Emperor and currently standing civilian government. The initial Postwar Surrender Policy, a modification of BLACKLIST, stated, "The Supreme Commander will exercise his authority through the Japanese governmental machinery and agencies, including the Emperor to the extent that this satisfactorily furthers United States Objectives."[19] BLACKLIST and MacArthur's overwhelming presence would form the starting point for reconstruction in postwar Japan.

Political Planning

As anyone who has been involved with creating a political solution to a problem might attest, fundamental differences between political and military planning tend to make political planning less energetic than military. Postwar planning in World War II was no exception to the generalization. Less organized and more European focused than military planning, political

---

November, 1944 from COL John E. Metzler. The memorandum was added as an addition to the final plan for Operation ECLIPSE.

[18] John Ray Skates, *The Invasion of Japan: Alternative to the Bomb*. (Columbia, SC: University of South Carolina Press, 2000), 167, 200.

[19] John Dower. *Embracing Defeat: Japan in the Wake of World War II*. (New York: W.W. Norton/ New Press, 1999), 212.

planning was characterized by a constant chafing of interests between the four main Allied

powers: United States, United Kingdom, France and the Soviet Union . In the United States,

while the cabinet was in disagreement over what to do with postwar Germany, President

Roosevelt stated in a memorandum to Secretary of State Cordell Hull, "I dislike making detailed

plans for a country which we do not yet occupy."[20] Toward Japan, Allied powers had little

interest. The Europe-first policy toward the war effort fostered the belief that ample time existed

in which to plan for postwar activities in Japan. With the exception of the Soviet Union, which

was attempting to position itself to gain from the dissolution of the Japanese Empire, the mantra

of unconditional surrender substituted for policy and postwar planning.

Although disagreement and discord pushed postwar planning into military hands until the

war was nearly finished, political leaders occasionally showed glimmers of thought for the future.

At the first Quebec conference in August 1943, Lieutenant General Morgan convinced Churchill

and Roosevelt to consider postwar Europe. Little additional guidance emerged until April 28,

1944, when the Combined Chiefs of Staff (CCS) released CCS/551, "Directive for the Military

Government in Germany Prior to Defeat or Surrender." CCS/551 gave the Supreme Commander,

Allied Powers Europe (SCAPE) the authority and responsibility for governing occupied

Germany. With the task for governance came the implied task to plan for the occupation. In

April 1945, as German resistance weakened, more guidance was handed to General Dwight D.

Eisenhower in the form of JCS 1067, which was designed to implement the Morgenthau Plan.

The Morgenthau Plan, formed by Secretary of the Treasury Henry Morgenthau, aimed at

ensuring Germany would never again be a military threat through the pastoralization of the

country. The basic objectives of JCS 1067 included elimination of Nazism and militarism,

---

[20] U.S. Department of State. *The United States and Germany, 1945-1955. Department of State Publication 5827.* (United States Government Printing Office: May, 1955), 5. Hereafter cited as DOS Pub 5827.

apprehension and punishment of war criminals, limited control of the German economy, disarmament and demilitarization, and an eventual reconstruction of a democratic political system. The provisions of JCS 1067 were presented to the other Allied Powers at the Potsdam Conference in July-August 1945 and were generally agreed upon by all.[21] As usual, the only thing to come out of Potsdam aimed at Japan was a reiteration the requirement for Japan's unconditional surrender.[22]

A proximate cause for the lack of planning for any occupation of Japan was the simple fact that planners believed they would have adequate time to prepare during the final phase of the campaign in the Pacific. Strategic planners in the Pacific expected at least another year before the final assault on the Japanese homeland followed by a lengthy campaign on the Japanese islands.[23] A longer lead time for planning would have allowed for the leisurely consideration of the issues involved in the future of Japan, and allowed them to build on the structure and lessons learned in the European theater.

Good planning did not ensure the occupation of Germany would be problem free. Despite the level of effort that went into European planning, problems were still identified, addressed, and fixed throughout the military governance in Germany. The plan did, however, create a framework, outline processes and procedures, and allocate resources for the occupation,

---

[21] DOS Pub 5827. Department of State Publication 5827 gives a detailed description of the planning effort in Europe. A description of the contents of JCS 1067 can be found in John L Snell. *Wartime Origins of the East West Dilemma Over Germany*. (New Orleans: The Hauser Press, 1958). Major Kenneth O. McCreedy does an excellent job of describing the military considerations involved in JCS 1067 in his monograph.

[22] *General HQ, Southwest Pacific.* Basic Outline Plan for "BLACKLIST" Operations to Occupy Japan Proper and Korea After Surrender or Collapse. *1945. (Hereafter cited as* BLACKLIST*)* This trend is continued into BLACKLIST, the plan for the occupation and control of the Japanese home islands. While BLACKLIST's European counterpart, ECLIPSE constantly reminds the reader of the strategic and political implications of all actions, BLACKLIST's basic plan gives little more than a set of maps and Logistical considerations. Strategic implications are largely ignored

[23] *BLACKLIST.* Although not explicitly stated in the plan, it is clear from the timelines and maps that planners expected at least one year to complete the plan. James Dobbins underscores the premise in *America's Role in Nation-Building: From Germany to Iraq.* (Santa Monica, CA: RAND, 2003) 32-33.

allowing the Allied forces to quickly and effectively address any disturbances that did occur. Possibly the most difficult and contentious portion of the plan for occupation of Germany was disposition of the war criminals. Would they be tried or simply shot? In either case, who should be blamed for the war?

If a trial was deemed necessary further questions became important. Who would conduct the trial? How would it be conducted? Where would it be conducted? What would be the purpose of the trial? The disposition of the prisoners and their subsequent trial became the focus of an intense political debate followed by concentrated military and civilian planning. Though the tribunal would eventually be established, it was through the perseverance and planning of two men, Secretary of State Henry Stimson and Supreme Court Justice Robert Jackson, that it found its character. The two men saw past the petty desire for revenge to champion the principle that the disposition of the prisoners and eventual conduct and outcome of a war trial would be the single greatest factor in determining the future of world peace.

WAR TRIALS—ERODING LEGITIMACY

> We want it to be fair. And of course, we want the world to say,
> well, this -- he got a fair trial. Because whatever justice is meted
> out needs to stand international scrutiny.
> -George W. Bush[24]

To a nation that has been under the rule of a tyrant for a generation or more, the idea of "rule of law" is difficult to conceive. Police are generally in place to ensure the continuance of the regime and satisfaction of the desires of political leaders. Courts are meant only to uphold the orders of those in charge; justice is what those in power say is appropriate. With the loss of belief in the rule of law comes fear, apathy, despair, and the search for something with which to impose order. Added to the disbelief in the good intent of law comes a constant lack of public safety. Policemen and their superiors do little to further the cause of safety unless it helps their own ends. The trust between the law enforcement officer and civilian is turned into wariness. A conviction that safety comes from one's own actions takes hold. If there is no external stimulus, the status quo will be maintained, lawlessness will prevail, public safety will be ignored, and justice forgotten.[25]

For a society in which the rule of law has been supplanted by the rule of thugs, restoration of rule of law has several components. First, to enforce the law, police forces must be trained and held to a legal, physical and moral standard. Second, a system of jurisprudence must be established to interpret and administer the law in the name of a duly appointed government. Third, a constitution and approved set of laws must be constructed, approved, and established. Finally, a corrections system judged as humane primarily by local standards, but acceptable

---

[24] George Bush. Press Conference, 15 December, 2003. Online at http://www.whitehouse.gov/news/releases/2003/12/20031215-3.html .

[25] Bard O'Neill. *Insurgency & Terrorism: Inside Modern Revolutionary Warfare*. (Washington DC: Brassey's Inc, 2001). 31-52.

internationally, must be instated.[26] Once the conditions have been met, the first necessity is to prove to the local population that the law means something. Simply having police on the corner is not new. People in most countries occupied by repressive ideological leadership have seen police presence for decades. Rounding up minor functionaries and petty criminals is likewise of little interest. Their removal from the system does little to change the overall functioning of society. What must be done to prove intent is to publicly present a fair trial and punishment of those responsible for the atrocities inflicted upon the population. Only then, when people feel they are safe to believe, will the beginnings of respect for the rule of law be internalized. With the belief that a new government can provide an environment that is safe and fair, the legitimacy of a government grows while that of an insurgency wanes. These problems are nothing new. Planners for postconflict World War II in both hemispheres were forced to contend with the same dilemma.

The Nuremberg Trials

At the conclusion of World War II, the prevailing opinion of those in charge of most Allied nations was that German war criminals should be found and executed as quickly as possible. Even in the United States, a faction led by Secretary of State Henry Morgenthau (and endorsed by General Eisenhower) advocated the summary execution of the leaders of the Nazi party.[27] The desire for revenge was perhaps understandable. The Nazi party had remorselessly

---

[26] Michele Fournoy, and Pan, Michael. "Justice and Reconciliation" Post Conflict Reconstruction Project, Center for Strategic and International Studies. Online at http://www.csis.org/isp/pcr/justicepaper. pdf. Accessed 3 December, 2003, Internet. The authors offer six pillars for postconflict reconstruction: law enforcement instruments that are effective and respectful of human rights; an impartial, open, and accountable judicial system; a fair constitution and body of law; mechanisms for monitoring and upholding human rights; a humane corrections system; and formal and informal reconciliation mechanisms for dealing with past abuses and resolving grievances arising from conflict. Some of the ideas espoused in the article are captured in this monographs requirements for a return to the rule of law.
[27] John L Snell. *Wartime Origins of the East West Dilemma Over Germany*. (New Orleans: The Hauser Press, 1958), 185-6.

perpetrated some of the most heinous crimes seen in war. Everyone on the European continent and British Islands had been directly affected in some way by the war; it would be difficult to find a person who had not lost a loved one to German aggression.

Fortunately, cooler heads were to be found in some high offices. Henry Stimson, Secretary of War for the United States, counseled, "the objective was to attain peace in the future, not punishment for its own sake."[28] Additionally, Soviet Premier Joseph Stalin insisted on war trials for both nations. When Harry S. Truman assumed the Presidency in April 1945, Morgenthau's influence waned and Stimson's waxed. Within a month, the American position became that the rule of law should be upheld. If the rule of law was to be upheld, there must be trials for those accused of war crimes. In August, representatives from the "Big Four"—Britain, France, United States, and the Soviet Union—met in London to create the London Charter of the International Military Tribunal, (Appendix 1) which would form the skeleton around which the Nuremberg Trials would grow.[29] The meeting became known as the London Conference.

Before the Nuremberg Tribunal, "international law" was a nebulous set of ideas and customs to which nations adhered when convenient. Attempts to codify international law included the Hague Conventions of 1899 and 1907 which focused on surrendered and captured combatants, and the Treaty of Paris, also known as the Kellogg-Briand Pact, in which war was outlawed. (Appendix 2) Although both were ratified by every major European power (including Germany), neither was blessed with the teeth to facilitate enforcement.[30] The Nuremberg trial would be the first modern international war trial planned and executed. As such, it would set the precedent not only for post WWII trials, but for all international war trials and tribunals in the

---

[28] Noel Annan. *Changing Enemies*. (New York: W.W. Norton & Company, 1996), 202.
[29] Telford Taylor. *Nuremberg and Vietnam: an American Tragedy*. (Chicago: Quadrangle Books, 1970), 81. Hereafter referred to as Taylor, *Nuremberg*.
[30] Telford Taylor. *The Anatomy of the Nuremberg Trials; A Personal Memoir*. (New York: Alford A. Knopf, 1992), 17-19. Hereafter referred to as Taylor, *Anatomy*.

future. Thus, one real goal of the Nuremberg trial was to make a statement in support of

international law.[31]

In addition to the necessity to foster international law, the Nuremberg trial was the most

visible manifestation of the process of "denazification" at all levels. As it was conceivable that

the greater part of the population of Germany had in some way been involved with Nazi

activities, it became necessary that potential criminals be categorized by the severity of their

crimes, tried and punished accordingly, with Nuremberg receiving only the worst war criminals

and leaders. [32] For success, the trial would have to be well documented, public, and

irreproachably fair.

The setting for the trials befitted its importance. In a presentation worthy of Hollywood,

the courtroom was a somber, wood paneled, cathedral-like room that perfectly underscored the

gravity of the situation. On one side of the room were the eight judges: one primary and one

alternate for each of the "big four" countries. On the other side, under the stern glare of tall,

muscular, crisply starched military policemen were twenty-one disheveled and bedraggled

formerly powerful men accused of monstrous crimes. In the no-man's land between the two

encampments were a battalion of court reporters and secretaries to record events for posterity and

tables for the defense counsel. Prosecutors looked on sternly from aside the assemblage while

bookending the gallery was a quiet cacophony of hurriedly scribbling reporters, quietly mumbling

interpreters, haughtily kibitzing VIPs, and incessantly rolling cameras. [33]

Into the sober setting strode Robert Jackson, a Supreme Court Justice and Chief

Prosecutor for the United States. He began eloquently, reminding all present that the trial was not

---

[31] Taylor, *Anatomy*. 81.
[32] *ECLIPSE*, Memorandum #19. The problem of numbers continued into the Tokyo tribunals in which a total of 5,700 individuals were indicted under the tiered system for Class B and C crimes. Dower, *Embracing Defeat*, 447.

merely about revenge or legal theories. It was, "the practical effort of four of the most mighty of nations, with the support of seventeen more, to utilize international law to meet the greatest menace of our time—aggressive war."[34] Building on his foundation of purpose, he continued that the intent of the trial was not to punish Germany, or the German people, but to expose the guilt of those people so evil as to order the atrocities perpetrated on the world. The barbaric acts, which were so odious as to make people in the room ill, included wholesale killing of Jews and Gypsies, destruction of the Warsaw Ghettoes, aggressive war starting with Poland and migrating all over Europe, mistreatment of Prisoners of War (POWs) and experimentation on other prisoners.[35]

As he concluded his remarks and solemnly returned to his bench, there was no doubt as to the direction the trial would take. From November 21st, 1945 until October 1st, 1946, while the world watched, twenty-one men and six organizations were tried on one or more of four charges: crimes against peace, crimes against humanity, war crimes, and conspiracy. (See Appendix 3 for definitions of the crimes) Fifteen days later, twelve men shuffled to the gallows to atone for their crimes. Martin Bormann, Adolf Hitler's private secretary and one of the most powerful Nazi leaders, was tried in absentia and sentenced to hang. Another, armament manufacturer Gustav Krupp von Bohlen, was judged too feeble to stand trial. As to the remaining defendants, three received life sentences, three were acquitted, and four received sentences ranging from ten to twenty years.[36] Despite (or perhaps because of) the gravity of the proceedings, questions as to the validity of the tribunal, judges, and processes began almost immediately.

---

[33] Michael R. Marrus. *The Nuremberg War Crimes Trial, 1945-46; A Documentary History*. (Boston: Bedford Books, 1997), 71-77.

[34] International Military Tribunal. "Second Day, Wednesday, 11/21/1945, Part 04", in Trial of the Major War Criminals before the International Military Tribunal. Volume II. Proceedings: 11/14/1945-11/30/1945. [Official text in the English language.] Nuremberg: IMT, 1947. pp. 98-102. Online at http://www.courttv.com/archive/casefiles/nuremberg/jackson.html. Accessed 18 January, 2004.

[35] Ibid.

[36] Marrus, 258-261.

One of the new concepts to come from the Nuremberg trials was the idea that leaders were responsible for the actions of their subordinates. Although the notion had some historical basis, in context, it was a new idea.[37] Also new was the prosecution of civilians, both governmental leadership and captains of industry; and entire organizations for their actions in support of war. Inconsistencies in who was tried raised questions. For example, Admiral Dönitz, commander of German submarine forces, was convicted of aggressive war yet his superiors were not. According to the argument made against Dönitz, all ship captains could be held accountable for aggressive war.[38] Yet most captains were allowed to remain free or serve short prison terms. Another consideration was whether or not Germans should have been included in the process of identifying, prosecuting and judging the guilty. The idea was rejected early in the process based on experience in WWI, but has remained in hindsight ever since. For the Germans to participate in the punishment of their own may have encouraged local perception that justice was fair and equitable to all.

If the implicit goal of the Nuremberg trial was to make a statement in favor of international law, the explicit goal was to show the guilt of the Nazis and deal a blow to the legitimacy of the movement. A vivid depiction of the depravity of their actions would crush internal and external support to the cause morally, monetarily, and physically.[39] The public nature of the trials graphically brought the actions of the defendants into the common man's

---

[37] Taylor, *Nuremberg*. 82-83. Also in John Rice. Famous Trials: The Trial of Captain Henry Wirz, Commandant Andersonville Prison, 1865. The UMKC School of Law Website. Online at http://www.law.umkc.edu/faculty/projects/ftrials/wirz/wirz.htm. [Internet]. Captain Henry Wirz was the Commandant of the confederate Andersonville Prison during the Civil War. During his time as Commandant, numerous prisoners died from wounds received at the hands of prison guards. Wirtz was tried for their actions. His trial and conviction set a precedent that superiors are responsible for the acts of their subordinates and was used as a precedent in post WWI and WWII trials. However, as the Civil War was largely ignored by European nations (Von Moltke reportedly told his officers to ignore it as it was of little significance) and post WWI trials were ineffective in conveying most messages, including the message of responsibility of the superiors, it can be debated that the Andersonville precedent was largely confined to the American interpretation of international law.
[38] Ibid, 86.

house, accomplishing the objective in an unprecedented manner. Upon completion of the trials, the world truly believed the Nazis were not only guilty, but despicable in their acts. The moral blow to the movement helped to prevent an uprising of support from people who thought the great leaders had been somehow wronged. In order to prevent future concerns about hidden agendas, the process was well documented. Upon completion, results were published in English and French (but not German) and released for public scrutiny.

The Tokyo Trials

It is difficult to characterize the Tokyo trials without comparing them to Nuremberg. Ostensibly, the Tokyo trials were to follow the example laid out in Europe. Reality was much different. The suddenness of the collapse of the Japanese Empire, cultural differences between the East and West, and primordial hatred of the Americans toward the Japanese combined with a desire to "get the war over with" to make the tribunal a pale facsimile of its progenitor. Legal systems, personnel, and coalitions with other nations were hastily established to facilitate the trial. Instead of a formal colloquium such as the London Conference in which goals and conduct of the trial were discussed, General MacArthur issued a decree ordering the trials and Joseph B. Keenan, who would eventually be the Chief Prosecutor, drew up the charter. Where Nuremberg had judges from four largely westernized nations, Tokyo laid claim to a bench representing eleven nations of differing cultures from around the globe, ensuring conflict within the court.[40]

Cultural differences guaranteed that definitions of right and wrong varied by nation. That which was considered a war crime under international and Western law could be considered good order and discipline in Japanese society. Accordingly, the application of Anglo-American law on Japanese culture proved difficult for the Japanese (and perhaps even some Justices) to

---

[39] O'Neill, 90-110.
[40] Minear,20, 23.

understand. Although the focus of the trials in Tokyo was on twenty-one men, the chasm in

belief led to an untenable number (greater than 50,000) of Japanese citizens convicted of crimes

of varying degrees. Over 900 men were executed with thousands convicted of lesser crimes in

numerous courts.[41]

Like Nuremberg, the setting of the trial attempted to represent the importance of the

proceedings. However, if Nuremberg was a Hollywood performance worthy of an Oscar, Tokyo

more resembled a "B" grade movie. The courtroom, which mimicked Nuremberg on a more

grandiose scale, was a large, dark paneled room custom made for the drama to be staged.   With

room for over 500 spectators and hundreds of court personnel, the chamber was so large that it

made the accused in the small prisoners' dock appear insignificant. Even the seemingly

untouchable judicial system was increased, with eleven justices and over 100 men working for

the prosecution. Justice B. V. A. Röling of the Netherlands later commented, "It was like a huge-

scale theatrical production."[42]

The trials opened, minus two justices, on May 3rd, 1946 not to a great series of orations,

but to a litany of motions questioning the validity of the trials. The first motion challenged the

legality of the trials in conjunction with the Potsdam Declaration and Instrument of Surrender.

(Appendix 4) The second challenged the validity of including several concepts under

international law including "aggressive war" the responsibility of an individual in war, and the

definition of "murder" in an aggressive war. A third, filed on behalf of four prisoners, claimed

violations of individual rights. All motions were dismissed within a week.[43] Beginning June 4th,

1946, the prosecution presented its case. For thirty-one months, until its close in April 1948, the

---

[41] John L. Ginn. Sugamo Prison, Tokyo, An Account of the Trial and Sentencing of Japanese War Criminals in 1948 by a U. S. Participant. (Jefferson, NC: McFarland & Company, 1992), 121-175. Also discussed in Minear, 172-4 and Dower, Embracing Defeat, 459.

[42] Dower, *Embracing Defeat*, 449, 461.

[43] Minear, 21-26.

trial ground through thousands of pages of documents and over 450 witnesses. The final verdict sent seven men to their death, sixteen to life sentences and one to a seven year sentence. [44]

Unlike Nuremberg, the final verdict was not unanimous; three justices filed dissenting opinions. Justice Henri Bernard of France dissented on both procedural grounds and the deletion of the Japanese emperor from the list of those indicted. Justice Radhabinod Pal of India wrote, in a 1,200 page dissenting opinion, that there was no proof of conspiracy, evidence was slanted in favor of the prosecution, war crimes were not proven, and aggressive war was not illegal under international law. Justice Röling questioned the concept of civilian responsibility for military acts, and, although he agreed in principle that aggressive war was a crime, questioned the political legality of the concept. The dissents were neither read nor published in the official record. Only Justice Pal's, which was published in India, found its way into immediate general circulation. The dissents, conduct of the trial, and omissions paved the way for immediate criticism of the trial. [45]

Also unlike the European model, many senior members of the Japanese government and military, to include the emperor, were not convicted (or even tried) for crimes. Although some senior Japanese personnel were tried, the majority of those who paid for the crimes were lower level functionaries. The discrepancy led to the belief in Japanese society that the lower classes were being made to pay for the failure of the upper classes. [46] The most questionable case was Emperor Hirohito. Implicit in the agreement made prior to surrender was that Hirohito would not be tried as a war criminal. The decision not to try the emperor was seen as beneficial to both parties. The United States needed someone to figurehead the government, establishing its

---

[44] Minear, 26. Also in Dower, 449.

[45] Dower, 457-461,

[46] Herbert P. Bix. *Hirohito and the Making of Modern Japan*. (New York: Harper Collins Publishers, 2000), 534-5.

legitimacy while the Japanese still believed in the divine nature of the emperor.[47] To prevent

uncomfortable questions as to his wartime conduct, the emperor was portrayed as a savior of

peace. Yet the position led to some awkward situations. For example, since the emperor could

not do wrong, those under him must have disobeyed his orders and conducted evil warlike acts;

but if the emperor was a god, why did he allow it to happen? If he was all knowing, how could

he be deceived? Even more awkward was the question of the divinity of the emperor. If the

emperor was a god, how could he be wrong? If he couldn't be wrong, how could it have been

illegal to follow his orders? Such questions were a direct result of Western powers' lack of

understanding of Oriental culture in general and Japanese culture in specific. The end result was

the perception that the seven men convicted and hanged at Tokyo became martyrs who died

shielding the emperor.[48]

A chink in the armor of Western law also appeared in the decision not to punish the

emperor. The Kellog-Briand pact of 1928 established an understanding that a nation goes to war,

not an individual. However, if the leadership of a nation is engendered in the face, words and

actions of a single godlike man, are not the actions of a nation merely an extension of his will?

Therefore, if a nation, under the leadership of a single individual goes to war, how can the leader

of that nation go unpunished? Adding even more friction to the problem was the question of the

legitimacy of the Kellogg-Briand pact. By declaring war illegal, the pact made an attack against

the concept of national sovereignty. If war is, in fact, an extension of national policy and will,

then to declare it illegal is to undermine the authority of the government of a nation. The

dilemma created a problem of Clausewitzian proportions.[49]

---

[47] Dower, Embracing Defeat, 212.
[48] Ibid, 461.
[49] Ibid, 464-5.

The exclusion of the emperor from the collection of those tried notwithstanding, the list was fundamentally flawed. At times, the list seemed to be a haphazardly constructed document reflecting the need to make a statement to Western powers that justice was being served. Atrocities that happened against Japanese citizens or Oriental powers were largely forgotten or ignored. Consequently, many of the worst offenders were not prosecuted. Examples of those omitted included the *kempetai*, ostensibly military police but actually thugs who often committed heinous acts against prisoners and civilians alike; those from big businesses and *kaizen*[50] who fanned the flames of war to engender personal profit; and military and civilian leaders who forced women into sex slavery as "comfort women," as well as sadistic researchers who experimented on prisoners and those who waged chemical warfare in China, both in violation of the Geneva accords. Lacunae of such magnitude only served to muddle the message of final justice being expounded by the tribunal.[51]

The legal process itself possessed innate flaws that implied the judgment and sentencing of those indicted was predetermined. On opening day of the trial, all was not in order. Two of the eleven justices were unaccounted for and there were only three translators for the defense; yet the trial commenced unrelentingly. Once all justices arrived, further discrepancies were apparent. One was a survivor of the Bataan death march who was clearly prejudiced against the Japanese and four were mere figureheads who were not even permitted to write their own opinions. Furthermore, the Soviet judge was actually a politician with no judicial experience and only one justice had any experience in international law. Broadening the lack of synergy on the bench, the eleven justices never met in consultation and rarely unanimously agreed on a verdict.[52]

---

[50] *Kaizen,* which translates to "betterment" or "improvement" were actually monopolistic companies that used their control of the market to better their position.

[51] Dower, Embracing Defeat, 470.

[52] Minear, 82.

Adding to the flawed appearance of the trial, records of the proceedings were inconsistently maintained and not fully published after the close of the trials, inviting questions as to its conduct and outcome. The trials were not as well publicized as Nuremberg, suggesting an indifference to world and local opinion. Finally, the concepts and prosecution of crimes against humanity and aggressive war presented a problem when the victors had arguably conducted similar crimes. The United States not only firebombed German and Japanese cities but dropped the atomic bomb on Hiroshima and Nagasaki leading to the deaths of thousands of civilians. The Red Army allowed 100,000 (mostly poor) Japanese civilians to die in Manchuria during the winter of 1945. Colonial powers had aggressively attempted to take over Asia long before Japan. The door was wide open for future critique of the process. [53]

---

[53] Discussed in Dower, *Embracing Defeat*, 456. The Russians were believed to have sentenced thousands of Japanese citizens in Manchuria, both military and civilian, to death and hard labor. Due to the closed nature of the Soviet Union at the time, accurate numbers cannot be discerned.

THE LEGACY OF NUREMBERG AND TOKYO

> "The law is a living, growing thing. In no other sphere is it more necessary to affirm that the rights and duties of States are the rights and duties of men and that unless they bind individuals they bind no one. It is a startling proposition that those who aid and abet, who counsel and procure the commission of a crime, are themselves immune from responsibility"
> -Sir Hartley Shawcross, Closing Speech at Nuremberg Trials [54]

Readdressing the Concept of International Law

The three concepts originally espoused at Nuremberg—crimes against peace, war crimes and crimes against humanity—were not groundbreaking concepts. One of the first complete and systematic outlines of what was and was not permissible in war was written by St. Thomas Aquinas in *Summa Theologica*. In his text, St. Thomas outlines proper justification for permissible activities in war. His ideas became the model for theorists through the ages and have become inculcated into the theory of just war. [55] Just war theory offers principles that erect a moral framework for the conduct of a just war (*Justum Bellum*). The two components of just war theory, *Jus ad Bellum*, the rules governing the conduct of war and *Jus in Bello*, the rules that govern fair conduct in combat, offer a moral compass for waging war.

Previously, the concepts of *Jus in Bello* and *Jus ad Bellum* were nebulous concepts, offering guidelines, but not erecting firm boundaries. Nuremberg and Tokyo served to codify the imprecise guidelines and traditions, creating a clear-cut classification of international law that delimited right and wrong. With new hindrances, there was bound to be some dissent. Alex Moseley, author of "Just War Theory" in the *Internet Encyclopedia of Philosophy* exposes the root of the problem. "Historically the just war tradition—a set of mutually agreed upon rules of

---

[54] Sir Hartley Shawcross. "Closing Comments." *The Trial of German Major War Criminals sitting at Nuremberg, Germany.* Vol.19 , Session 187 (pp.423-428), 26 July 1946.
[55] Alex Moseley. "Just War Theory." *Internet Encyclopedia of Philosophy*. James Fieser, General Editor. Online at http://www.utm.edu/research/iep/j/justwar htm.

combat—commonly evolves between two similar enemies. When enemies differ greatly because of different religious beliefs, race, or language, war conventions have rarely been applied."[56]

Conflicting opinions and criticism of the trials often centered on the differences among the races. Although written for the Tokyo tribunal, Justice Pal's dissent contained the overarching (and most commonly cited) discrepancies of the two trials. His argument began by considering the validity of the crimes. If the crimes had not been established as crimes in international law prior to their commission, how could they be tried as crimes after their commission? The consideration of *ex post facto* (after the fact) law exposed a real inconsistency in the trails. Every country that advocates democratic principles has rules preventing the application of *ex post facto law*. For justices of countries that ascribe to such fundamental beliefs to completely disregard the concept undermines the very legitimacy of the trial. Building on the first question, Pal continued by questioning the legality of the tribunal to try the crimes. If the crimes were not international law, the tribunal was legislating law from the bench; a privilege to which Pal felt the tribunal was not entitled. Finally, the question of legality of *ex post facto* law brought with it the taint of victor's justice. If crimes were to be codified and judged after the fact, then all potential commissioners of war crimes should be tried—including the United States and Soviet Union—not just the loser of the war.

The concept of aggressive war erected an additional stumbling block. Who was to say what is aggressive and what is simply national policy? Similarly, who was privileged to give a definition of crimes against peace? Historically, the victor had always been accorded the prerogative. Therefore, at the end of WWII when Germany and Japan lay prostrate to the benevolence of the Allied Powers, any mercy meted out to the vanquished was the prerogative of the Allies by right of arms. Any concessions to justice or even common decency were at the

---

[56]Ibid.

discretion of the Allied Powers. Two further considerations involved the rules of evidence (who and what was admissible in court), and the concept of negative criminality[57], the idea that those in charge have a binding responsibility to prevent criminal atrocities. Clearly, international law as a codified and enforceable set of laws was still had room for evolution.

Evolution of International Law Since WWII

In October 1945 the United Nations was born with the stated purpose: "to maintain international peace and security; to develop friendly relations among nations; to cooperate in solving international economic, social, cultural and humanitarian problems and in promoting respect for human rights and fundamental freedoms; and to be a centre for harmonizing the actions of nations in attaining these ends."[58] The framers of the original charter of the United Nations realized that to facilitate the lofty goals of the fledgling organization, they must institute a means by which member nations could peacefully resolve their differences. Building on the foundation of the Permanent Court of International Justice previously associated with the League of Nations, the UN established the International Court of Justice (ICJ) in 1946. The ICJ would

---

[57] United Nations War Crimes Commission. *Law Reports of Trials of War Criminals. Selected and Prepared by the United Nations War Crimes Commission.* Volume IV. London: HMSO, 1948. [online] http://www.ess.uwe.ac.uk/genocide/trials.htm. Accessed 15 April, 2004. The event that established internationally the concept that a superior does have a responsibility to prevent illegal events was the trial of General Tomoyuki Yamashita, who was tried and condemned by a United States Military Commission in Manila. In an appeal that made it to the United States Supreme Court, he stated that he had not personally committed or directed the acts which were the subject of the charges. Although the Supreme Court did not rule directly upon the charges, it did state that the commission must consider, "evidence tending to establish the culpable failure of petitioner to perform the duty imposed on him by the law of war and to pass upon its sufficiency to establish guilt." Accordingly, the commission charged Yamashita with failure to properly execute his duties as army commander to control the operations of the members of his command by permitting them to commit,"the extreme and widespread atrocities specified," and subsequently sentenced to death.

[58] United Nations Website. Online at http://www.un.org/aboutun/basicfacts/unorg.htm. The site states, "In 1945, representatives of 50 countries met in San Francisco at the United Nations Conference on International Organization to draw up the United Nations Charter. The Organization officially came into existence on 24 October 1945, when the Charter had been ratified by China, France, the Soviet Union, the United Kingdom, the United States and a majority of other signatories. United Nations Day is celebrated on 24 October"

become the "primary judicial organ"[59] of the UN. The stated role of the ICJ is, "to settle in

accordance with international law the legal disputes submitted to it by States, and to give advisory

opinions on legal questions referred to it by duly authorized international organs and agencies."[60]

With the acknowledgment by member states of the United Nations that the ICJ was

supposed to settle disputes in accordance with international law came a requirement to establish

some form of international law; a circular conundrum that created another hurdle for international

justice. Creation of binding international law required a nation to give up a portion of its

sovereignty—an obviously unpopular necessity. Since no nation would be likely to give up a

modicum of its own sovereignty, international law could never be codified under the auspices of

the ICJ. The website of the International Law Commission of the United Nations sums up the

problem.

> The Governments participating in the drafting of the Charter of the United Nations were
> overwhelmingly opposed to conferring on the United Nations legislative power to enact
> binding rules of international law. As a corollary, they also rejected proposals to confer in
> the General Assembly the power to impose certain general conventions on States by
> some form of majority vote. There was, however, strong support for conferring on the
> General Assembly the more limited powers of study and recommendation, which led to
> the adoption of the following provision in article 13, paragraph 1: "The General
> Assembly shall initiate studies and make recommendations for the purpose of: a.
> Encouraging the progressive development of international law and its codification."[61]

The organization created to promote the development of international law was the International

Law Commission or ILC.

---

[57] The United Nations International Court of Justice Registry of the Court. *International Court of Justice Website*. Online at http:// www.icj-cij.org. The referenced page can be found at http://www.icj-cij.org/icjwww/igeneralinformation/icjgnnot html.

[60] Ibid.

[61] Codification Division, Office of Legal Affairs, United Nations. *United Nations International Law Commission*. Online at http://www.un.org/law/ilc/introfra.htm. Hereafter referred to as *ILC*.

On January 31, 1947, the General Assembly of the United Nations adopted resolution 94 (I), establishing the ILC. Not designed to be a judicial organization, its purpose, stated in Article 1, paragraph 1, of the Statute of the International Law Commission is:

> The promotion of the progressive development of international law and its codification." Article 15 of the Statute makes a distinction "for convenience" between progressive development as meaning "the preparation of draft conventions on subjects which have not yet been regulated by international law or in regard to which the law has not yet been sufficiently developed in the practice of States" and codification as meaning "the more precise formulation and systematization of rules of international law in fields where there already has been extensive State practice, precedent and doctrine.[62]

The single most key word in the statute is "draft." The fundamental statute of the ILC recognizes that international law cannot be binding without the support and consent of all international players. What it does provide is a generally recognized baseline of principles to which member states agree to conform.

One of the first accomplishments of the ILC was the *Draft Declaration of Rights and Duties of States* in 1949. In the document, rights of states are clearly articulated, granting every state equality, sovereignty, and the right to self defense (Appendix 5). The next year the ILC codified what had been learned in Nuremberg in the *Principles of International Law Recognized in the Charter of the Nuremberg Tribunal and in the Judgment of the Tribunal.*[63] The *Principles* addressed many of the problems exposed in the criticism of the Nuremberg trials and dissents of the Justices of the Tokyo trials to include crimes against peace, war crimes, crimes versus humanity and negative criminality. The *Draft Code of Offences against the Peace and Security of Mankind*, also known as the *Code of Crimes* was created in 1954 to provide further definition,

---

[62] ILC, *Statute of the International Law Commission.* Online at http://www.un.org/law/ilc/texts/ statufra htm.
    [63] ILC, *Principles of International Law Recognized in the Charter of the Nürnberg Tribunal and in the Judgment of the Tribunal. Online at* http://www.un.org/law/ilc/texts/nurnfra.htm.

and updated in 1996 to add modernizing concepts.[64] The baseline for international law had been set based on precedents from Germany and Japan. All that was missing was a set of teeth to enforce the laws.

Since its inception, the UN has struggled with the necessity to have some international body to enforce criminal law. Although the ILC was established as the primary judicial arm of the United Nations, it was not intended to try criminal cases. Usually, cases have been decided in ad hoc courts created specifically for the occasion such as the International Criminal Tribunal for the former Yugoslavia (ICTY), and the International Criminal Tribunal for Rwanda (ICTR). The ICTY was established by Security Council resolution 827 to deal with "serious violations of international humanitarian law committed in the territory of the former Yugoslavia since 1991, and as a response to the threat to international peace and security posed by those serious violations."[65] Its objectives were specifically set for a geographic region during a specified time sanctioned by a majority of member states of the United Nations. On November 8, 1994 the Security Council created the ICTR with stated purpose of:

> prosecution of persons responsible for genocide and other serious violations of international humanitarian law committed in the territory of Rwanda between 1 January 1994 and 31 December 1994. It may also deal with the prosecution of Rwandan citizens responsible for genocide and other such violations of international law committed in the territory of neighbouring [sic] States during the same period. The purpose of this measure is to contribute to the process of national reconciliation in Rwanda and to the maintenance of peace in the region.[66]

In addition to specificity in region and time, the most obvious similarity of the two tribunals is the humanitarian undertone of preventing genocide. With the establishment of the two tribunals, the

---

[64]*ILC. Draft Code of Offences against the Peace and Security of Mankind, 1954* . http://www.un.org/law/ilc/texts/offfra htm.

[65]Internet Unit of the Public Information Services (P.I.S.) of the ICTY. *The ICTY at a Glance*. In *United Nations International Criminal Tribunal for Yugoslavia Website*. Online at http://www.un.org/ icty/index html. Referenced page can be accessed at http://www.un.org/icty/glance/index.htm.

[66] ICTR Internet Task Force. United *Nations International Criminal Tribunal for Rwanda Website*. Online at http://www.ictr.org/default htm.

UN opened doors that had been left shut for a long time—prosecution of criminals for crimes against humanity.

As early as 1948, the General Assembly acknowledged the concept of genocide and the necessity for some form of action. However, inconsistencies in the definition of genocide and fear of ceding some portion of sovereignty to deal with the issue prevented further action. For over forty years the matter smoldered until it could no longer be ignored. Growing concerns about international drug trafficking and genocide forced the United Nation to reignite the debate, culminating in the creation of the International Criminal Court (ICC).[67] On February 25th, 2003 89 countries ratified the Rome Statute of the International Court to officially establish the ICC.

Despite the apparently mature state of international law, the field is still extremely politically charged. Before one nation attempts to try leaders or former leaders of another, it must consider the social and political ramifications of the venture. Nowhere is the fact more apparent than in current day Iraq. Cultural, religious, and political rifts threaten to undermine any efforts to bring the former heads of the Ba'ath party to justice. With the capture of the majority of the former Iraqi leadership, including Saddam Hussein, came a looming necessity for a trial of some form, under some auspices, with some result. To begin to fill in the blanks of what the trial should look like, one must compare the potential trial in Iraq to the events that spawned much of what is currently accepted international law—the Nuremberg and Tokyo Trials—and attempt to glean lessons for application in the new millennium.

---

[67] *Rome Statute of the International Criminal Court* in *Website of the International Criminal Court.* Online at URL: http://www.icc-cpi.int/php/show.php?id=home&l=EN. Referenced page is at URL: http://www.un.org/law/icc/general/overview htm. Accessed 19 February 2004. Internet.

IMPLICATIONS FOR IRAQ

> The Allied Forces serving under my command have entered
> Germany. We come as conquerors, but not as oppressors. In the
> area of Germany occupied by the forces under my command, we
> shall obliterate Nazi-ism [sic] and German Militarism
> -General of the Army Dwight D. Eisenhower.[68]

Whether similarities exist between post WWII Germany and post Operation Iraqi

Freedom is debatable. What should be apparent is that there are lessons to be learned from the

trials. Not only were they the most successful war trials in world history, but they forced the

United Nations to set a standard for international law and became the model for the standard.

Looking at history for a clue of what to expect in the future, Nuremberg and Tokyo become the

point of departure for modeling a modern trial. From the start of planning, one can hear echoes of

WWII in Operation Iraqi Freedom.

Planning for Success

Original planning for the United States invasion of Iraq in 2003 called for over 130 days

of combat action. When executed, the actual time taken to reach Baghdad was considerably less.

Similarly, the speed with which the Taliban government of Afghanistan fell in 2002 surprised

many planners.[69] A lack of consideration for "what comes next" due to a quicker than expected

campaign may have prevented real investigation into the problems that would be incurred with

post conflict operations. The suddenness with which both countries were defeated was

reminiscent of Japan.

---

[68] Dwight D. Eiseinhower. quoted in, The General Board, United States Forces, European Theater. *Procedures Followed by Civil Affairs and Military Government in the Restoration, Reorganization, and Supervision of Indigenous Civil Administration.* SHAEF, 17 June, 1945. p.17.
[69] Author's conversation with COL Kevin Benson, Director, School for Advanced Military Studies. Formerly Coalition Forces, Land Component Command (CFLCC) C5 (Plans) during Operation Iraqi Freedom.

Regardless of the level of planning undertaken for an event, planners must stand ready to conquer unexpected eventualities. Although it is too late to rectify the problems inherent in a missed planning opportunity, force of personality combined with a focus on future operations as well as current developments can lessen their impact.

Legitimacy

It is impossible to eliminate the legitimacy of the leadership of a nation unless the population of a nation acknowledges the legitimacy of the occupying force, government, or organization. Without the acceptance of the new government by the populace, the occupiers will simply be perceived as the same as the old boss. Before attempting the task, a few other considerations must be addressed.

A nation must ensure it has support of the international community. Without international support, the old regime has a legitimate grievance against the occupying nation. The former Ba'athists will likely attempt to portray themselves as victims of American aggression, giving the ideologue (or opportunist in the case of true Ba'athists) additional impetus to attack occupying forces. Mitigating their ability to portray themselves as martyrs to imperialism should be a top priority. A clear goal and agreement on the steps that would be taken in conduct of the trial in Germany led Allied powers to a verdict that was deemed fair and largely unbiased. Conversely, trials in Japan were seen as hasty, unilateral constructs biased toward American desires from the beginning to the final verdict. When conducting trials in Iraq, it may be convenient to use a coalition or United Nation judiciary to conduct the trials to attempt some legitimacy for the proceedings. The United States must realize that in attempting to legitimize the trials through international cooperation, it also engenders the potential for international discord on the final outcome. Alternatively, for the United States to conduct the trial under its own auspices would certainly provoke a negative reaction from the international community no matter what the verdict.

Application of Law

Legal and law enforcement communities must ensure consistent application of all laws, proceedings, and practices. Rules must be understood by the population and in accordance with local customs and traditions. Although Iraqi representation on the court may help in this bent, authorities must consider if the outcome will be acceptable. For instance, Iraq has a functioning government with an existing bureaucracy in place. Within the government, the country has a constitution and legal codes. Although the trust of the Iraqi people in the rule of law has been eroded, legal codes could be utilized with minimal immediate changes to establish legitimate government and rule of law, later to be modified as the new regime matures. [70]

A law that is not consistent with the norms of the society will be misunderstood and perceived as arbitrary and unenforceable by the Iraqi population. As obvious as the statement might seem, it is filled with layers of complexity that must be considered before a trial can proceed. First, what are the norms of society in Iraq? Although ostensibly a Muslim nation, the years of rule by Saddam Hussein have supplanted any message of Islamic law that may have been left over from previous rulers. Those past rulers were forced to contend with a nation artificially and arbitrarily constructed by the British from varying tribes and cultures carved out of the Ottoman Empire after the First World War. As an artificial construct, it is questionable if Iraqi society ever possessed a cultural identity with an attached set of values and norms. If it did, since an entire generation of Iraqis has grown up knowing only life under a dictator, Hussein's government likely supplanted those Iraqi norms.

Assuming a lack of extant cultural identity, to define the society one must look to the past. As a country, Iraq is an artificial conglomeration of tribes and cultures that has been under

---

[70] Frederick D. Barton and Bathsheba N. Crocker. *A Wiser Peace: An Action Strategy for a Post Conflict Iraq.* Washington D.C.: Center for Strategic and International Studies. January, 2003. Online at http://www.csis.org/isp/wiserpeace.pdf. Accessed 3 December, 2003, Internet.

the rule of a tyrant or king for the greater part of the last century. Before that, it was a part of the Ottoman Empire and the greater Arab culture. Parts of the Ottoman Empire can be forwarded as a model for positive Iraqi norms by emphasizing its cultural and scientific achievements while deemphasizing its militaristic tendencies. With an emphasis on emphasizing the lost glory of Iraq while vividly displaying the wretched conditions brought on by Saddam Hussein and the *Ba'ath* party, the Coalition can begin to marginalize the norms that have been inculcated in the society in the past twenty-five years.

Next, the Coalition must find some societal constant that the Iraqis can incorporate as the core of the "new—old values." Once again, the process requires a return to the past. Iraq, taken as a whole, is not far removed from a tribal society with tribal values. In the cities, the values are remembered. Outside the cities, they are actively practiced. One of the guiding principles is a deep respect for the elders of society. To capitalize on the respect of the Iraqis for their elders, the Coalition must find sympathetic elders and encourage them to remind younger Iraqis of the customs and traditions of past. With the aid of the elders comes the reminder that there were some values that all members of society held as important. Those positive values that coincide with the message of the coalition must be emphasized by the coalition to strengthen the concept of a societal norm and further the mission of a return to law.

The danger in the approach is the possibility of unsolicited elders opposed to the Coalition and direction in which Iraq is moving achieving demagogue status and actively working against Coalition efforts. To counter them, the Coalition must find a set of values to which all members of the nation will subscribe. The answer will come, in some shape, from Islam. Although Islam has fractured into competing sects, at its heart are a set of rules that combined with the glory of the past and a good information operations campaign can be the core of a new Iraqi cultural identity. Espousal of the Iraqi people as both descendants of an empire of artists and scholars and followers of a religion of peace and brotherhood could be the foundation of an organized campaign to shape the positive perception of the nation toward the trial process.

Perception

The entire trial process from concept to completion must be as transparent as possible. The Tokyo tribunal demonstrated the problems inherent in a trial in which the public perception of secret agendas, protocols and deals was rampant. Whether true or not, what the public perceives will quickly be understood as reality. Therefore, through the entire trial, there must be no appearance of impropriety. Recordkeeping of all processes including pre trial conferences, meetings, the trial itself, and disposition after the trial must be thorough, public, and published in as many languages as necessary to ensure the message is understood. Although open record keeping is no guarantee of a lack of mistrust, closed and incomplete records will bring suspicion upon the process. Justices must take elaborate precautions to ensure there is never any question of misconduct. The power of public perception should always be foremost in the mind of all participants

Capitalizing on the power of perception, atrocities and war crimes of the former regime must be made very apparent and public. Pictures and witnesses should be used for maximum shock effect to show both the world and people of the country, that what happened in the former regime was morally bankrupt. The intent should not only be to show the Iraqi people, but the entire world the perniciousness of the former regime. Loss of the moral high ground enjoyed by Saddam Hussein will endanger international support in the form of money, personnel, equipment and moral support and help lead to the death of an insurgency through its own weight. In addition, the right people must be prosecuted. Simply prosecuting the lower ranking members of an organization without consideration of their chiefs undermines the process and could create martyrs.

The bottom line

In all actions, we must consider the perception of the Iraqi people. The primary goal of the United States must be to do everything in its power to reduce the fear of the people of the nation. A war trial will be the first visible display of the American commitment to do so and a return to a "new normalcy" and rule of law. As people believe they are safe from the oppression of the past and begin to believe in the ability of the new government to provide for such a basic need as security, its status and legitimacy will grow. As there will be no chance to recover from an initial error in perception, the process must be done right the first time. Therefore, it behooves the creator to learn from the past for lessons. Once complete, the government will be able to concentrate on further areas to strengthen its legitimacy in the eyes of the people such as economic growth, education and reeducation.

A MODERN NUREMBERG?

"Ladies and Gentlemen, We got him."
-Paul Bremer[71]

In December 2003, American soldiers captured Saddam Hussein. With his capture came the conundrum of what to do next. Would he and his cronies be tried by the Iraqi people as a criminal, by the United States or Coalition as a war criminal or under the auspices of the United Nations and the ICC for crimes against humanity? Codification of international law and establishment of an international court would lead one to believe the ICC would hold the trial. Such a course of action might not be in the cards for Mr. Hussein. Ongoing attempts at justice by organs of the United Nations have proven to be almost comical. Beset by political grandstanding, finger pointing and accusations of victors' justice, the Yugoslavian and Rwandan trials have degraded into an ineffective farce of international justice. The United States is reluctant to enter into an agreement to try Hussein in such an environment. Initial indications suggested that the Iraqis might be offered the chance to bring Hussein to trial, but a lack of judicial infrastructure combined with the capriciousness of Iraqi politics preclude the ability of the United States to ensure the desired outcome of the trial—clearly an undesirable position. The remaining option is for the United States and its coalition partners to try Hussein themselves. Assuming a coalition trial as the most desirable option, what should such a trial look like?

To begin, the purpose of a trial must be considered. In a press conference on December 15th, 2003, President Bush was asked what the desired outcome for a trial would be. His response was that it must be fair and "withstand international scrutiny."[72] A trial meant to accomplish such a task would be a simple process; adhere to published international law and everything should

---

[71] Paul Bremer, *Text of Ambassador Bremer's Opening Remarks at the CPA Conference Center, Baghdad, December 14th, 2003*. Coalition Provisional Authority Website. Online at URL http://www.cpa-iraq.org/. The specifically referenced page can be found at URL http://www.cpa-iraq.org/ transcripts/ 20031214_Dec14_Saddam_Capture.htm. Accessed 4 March, 2004, [Internet].

come out as desired. The reality is significantly different. International, internal, and coalition politics as well as religious and ethical norms, must be addressed. Although the president's stated purpose for a trial is to withstand international scrutiny, American actions and statements throughout the conflict from prewar rhetoric to current statements have emphasized the common good for the local and international community, preservation of peace, and necessity to enforce UN mandates. Therefore, a better purpose might be, as Justice Jackson stated, "part of the great effort to make the peace more secure."[73] A better state of peace is significantly different than withstanding international scrutiny. Not only does it entail an adherence to international law, it requires contemplation of more amorphous concepts like fairness, perception, and belief. The necessity to influence the opinion of the international community to believe that conditions have improved in Iraq requires significantly more in depth planning, beginning with the principles and construct upon which the trials would be based.

International Law?

The most obvious and likely principle upon which the trials should be based is international law as espoused and codified by the United Nations. The documents agreed upon by the member states of the UN are meant to be a baseline for international justice. Despite apparent agreement, UN accords are little more than compromises describing the consensus of a committee. Accordingly, they rarely take into account specifics to the region or the peculiar beliefs of member nations such as considerations of religion, history, and local law. As learned in the Tokyo trials, if the people of a nation do not understand the laws under which their former leaders are tried, the outcome may not be considered fair by citizens of the state. Since difficulties involved with satisfying the desires of all nations are almost insuperable, the United

---

[72] George Bush. Press Conference, 15 December, 2003.
[73] International Military Tribunal. "Second Day, Wednesday, 11/21/1945, Part 04."

States must concentrate on the immediate problem: satisfying the desire of the people of Iraq for justice. If the citizens of the country are satisfied, the international community has little recourse but to accept the decision.

A possibility that must be considered is the application of *Sharia* or Muslim law. Incorporating the beliefs and norms inculcated by the Muslim faith could alleviate the local problem of understanding the "why" of law and bring Iraqis to the side of the United States. The dilemma inherent in the use of *Sharia* law is western perception. Muslim law is (obviously) religiously based, extreme, and not well understood by Western nations. The religious base flies in the face of one of the fundamental beliefs of United States, separation of church and state, and could create friction within the country. Although the government has chosen to ignore the opinions of other nations in dealings with Iraq in the past, political leaders ignore the feelings of their constituents at their own risk—especially in an election year. The extremity and strangeness of *Sharia* law could also create a stumbling block in its use in an Iraqi trial. As a very ancient form of law, many codes and punishments are perceived as medieval by western standards and pose a possible point of contention within the United States and other coalition partners.

In its most basic form, just war theory appears to be of little help. *Justum Bellum* deals primarily with nation states and their communication through war. The model gives little consideration to matters strictly within the borders of a nation. However, reading deeper into the principles of just war theory invites the possibility that intervention is justified in matters of self-determination. If a nation is not providing for its people, has harmed its people, or has disaffected its people and those same people have decided change is necessary, external force may be justified; a sticky point, but one that cannot be ignored. Belief in a just cause, internally to Iraq and the United States as well as externally to the rest of the world, should be a cornerstone of any international trial. Any model of justice that promotes such a conviction should somehow be integrated into the tenets of the trial.

A War Crimes Tribunal

Clearly, one set of rules or principles will not always fit the situation. Perhaps the most significant lesson that can be learned from the Nuremberg trials came from the London Conference. Held in late summer, 1945, the Conference was intended to ensure the four largest Allied nations—United States, United Kingdom, USSR, and France—were in agreement toward the disposition of war criminals after WWII. It culminated in early August, three months before the start of the Nuremberg Trials, with the London Agreement. The London Agreement established an International Military Tribunal and clearly delineated who, under what law, and how defendants would be tried. More importantly, in informal sessions of the Conference, representatives of the four nations that would try the Nazi war criminals ironed out many of the potential problems they would face in its conduct. Additionally, participants in the Conference engineered a framework around which to structure the trial, allowing all four members to present a unified façade during the process. No such conference was even attempted for the Tokyo Trials, resulting in discord on the bench and within the international community as to its conduct and outcome.

For the United States to simply offer a set of procedures and laws under which its enemies might be tried invites future criticism and accusations of victor's justice. Conversely, allowing the laws and procedures to be created by a committee could result in rules dominated by political agendas or so watered down as to mean little. The best case lies somewhere in the middle. The framers of a trial for Iraqi war criminals have the difficult task of constructing a set of rules and laws and procedures that incorporate just war theory and *Sharia* law under the umbrella of international law and still fulfill national, international and local Iraqi needs.

Participants in the conference must be from nations closely tied to the United States that have been in some way involved in the war. Although it is paramount that all countries appear to have no preconceived notions as to the outcome and a real voice in the process, in reality, all must have a singular focus in the conduct and conclusion of the trial. However, on no occasion should the United States be perceived as more than an equal in the trial. Staunch allies such as the United Kingdom and Australia should be invited to attend, but will be perceived internationally as puppets of the United States. To prevent the international view that the conference was a sham, intended to present the results of the trial *fait accompli* to the rest of the participants, organizers must ensure other countries, less tied to the United States are invited. Invited countries should be strong enough to have a presence internationally and be outwardly unfettered by relationships with the United States, yet have similar beliefs as the United States. Possible candidates include Poland, a former Warsaw Pact member that supported the war in Iraq, is supportive of the United States without being overwhelmingly so and has a desire to play a greater part in NATO; Albania, a Muslim country and former member of the Soviet Union that participated in the attack to Baghdad in Operation Iraqi Freedom; and France. Although not a participant in Operation Iraqi Freedom, France is a member of NATO, a participant in continuing military operations in Afghanistan, a nation with a large Muslim population,[74] and most importantly, a nation almost ubiquitously internationally perceived as not being a puppet of the United States.

Another possible candidate for inclusion is a representative from the United Nation. The inclusion of the UN could aid in increasing the positive international perception of the trials by directly involving the organization most responsible for international law and indirectly co-opting all member nations of the UN. Addition of the UN would not only help strengthen the legitimacy of the process, but also allow the legal organs of the UN to recapture prestige lost by the ICTY and ICTR while mending fences and bringing the UN closer to the Coalition.

---

[74] As of 1994, France had over 5 million persons of Muslim descent living in the country. Nationmaster.com. *Demographics of France*. [online] http://www.nationmaster.com/encyclopedia/ Demographics-of-France. Accessed 15 April 2004.

Since the results of an initial conference for the trial of Iraqi war criminals should consider international, *Sharia* and Western law along with just war theory to create a framework for the conduct of the trial, an additional consideration would be to include representatives of the Iraqi government to present the internal position. Therefore, when the conference begins, six nations: United States, United Kingdom, Australia, Poland, Albania, and France; the United Nations, and the Provisional (or possibly elected depending on the timeline) Iraqi Government should be sitting at the negotiation table.

The Trial

Once the framework of law has been blueprinted, more specific procedures for the daily physical conduct of the trial must be considered. Tokyo and Nuremberg gave the world a preview of the importance of setting and conduct when holding an international event. Famous trials and tribunals since then have simply underscored the importance of perception on the outcome of a trial. Several areas must be fully explored to exploit the informational and psychological possibilities inherent in such a huge undertaking.

Location

Post World War II trials also capitalized on the power of geographical location to further advance the message that was being forwarded. Trials held in Nuremberg, the location of many of Adolf Hitler's most fiery speeches, and Tokyo, the physical center of Japanese culture, visibly displayed that the regimes were finished forever. Recent UN trials have taken a different course with disappointing results. Meant to further the prestige of the UN, trials in Rwanda and Yugoslavia trials were held in The Hague, Netherlands. The ineffectiveness of the trials and lack of local information about the trials have had a contrary effect. Tied so closely to such an unproductive set of trials, the international image and reputation of the UN judicial capability has been severely damaged. Additionally, lack of information within the countries in which the crimes were committed make the actions of the UN seem far away.

It would be convenient for the American victors to hold the trial in the United States. Such a convenience would come at the cost of the support of the Arab states including Iraq. America is already seen as a powerful nation and needs no further assistance in enhancing the perception. Taking the criminals away for trial could create suspicion that something was being hidden, access was being denied, or justice was being predetermined. The ideal location for trial would be a place that holds a symbolic meaning to the people of the nation much like Nuremberg and Tokyo. Although Baghdad, as the former seat of *Ba'ath* power stands out as an obvious choice, a better choice may be Hussein's boyhood town, and perennial insurgent safe haven of Tikrit. A successful trial in the midst of what is currently a hotbed of insurgent activity would underscore the impotence of those still supporting the old *Ba'ath* regime and further enhance the position of the United States as a stabilizing power bent on reestablishing the rule of law in Iraq. Despite its desirable qualities, security problems involved in an unstable environment render the situation untenable. Securing a small city like Tikrit would be nearly impossible. Securing Baghdad would be completely impossible.

A choice that compromises between the symbolic power of Baghdad and Tikrit and the accessibility of the United States must be found. One possibility is to use Paris. In a trial, French opposition to the invasion of Iraq would be beneficial. The country is a leader in modern Europe and clearly not a pawn of the United States, yet its western value system is similar to that of the United States and would likely facilitate a judgment that is in accordance with American desires. Symbolically, Paris has long been viewed as a city of intelligentsia, peace, and reconciliation. Practically, the city is one of the most accessible in Europe and possesses readily available facilities. Legally, removal of the trial from Iraq erases any embarrassing questions of local sovereignty that could arise with the United States holding trial on an Iraqi citizen in a sovereign

Iraqi nation. Politically, use of Paris could heal ailing relations between France and the United States, in effect adding France to the Coalition after cessation of major combat operations in Iraq.

Setting

The first consideration is the setting. Remembering that the trial will be an international event, the setting must be arranged to take advantage of the occasion to further the message the Coalition is attempting to forward. To begin, the physical layout of the courtroom is of paramount importance. Both post WWII trials demonstrated that the design of the courtroom and presentation of the prisoners can be optimized to make the guilty look insignificant while enhancing the position of those in charge. Additionally, the trials showed the necessity to be careful not to offend the sensibilities of the locals by displaying their countrymen in a manner inconsistent with the norms of their culture. Location and access of the press can also be influential. The opportunity to position the press for the most dramatic effect and attempt to influence their perception of the trial is an opportunity that cannot be overlooked. Before placing the press, public affairs personnel must consider who will be invited to cover the trial. To only invite western journalists would create extreme distrust among the Arab nations. At a minimum, *Al-Jazeera*, the acknowledged leader in Middle Eastern journalism, must be present along with media from other countries not necessarily friendly to the Coalition. Additionally, C-SPAN, or a similar media organization should be permanently stationed at the trial to provide internationally accessible, real time coverage with no commentary, commercial, or political overtones.

Selection of Justices

Obviously, to try the prisoners, a set of justices is necessary. As with other considerations, who sits on the bench and tries the defendants is a decision not to be undertaken without substantial thought. Lessons from Nuremberg and Tokyo give insight into what must be taken into account when making the decision. First, the justices must appear free of personal prejudice. Although judges at Nuremberg were from the victorious nations, they maintained the appearance of impartiality. Tokyo presented a much different case. The difficulty involved with the appearance of impartiality in a modern trial begins to appear insurmountable. Most people and nations have taken some stance on the war in Iraq and the status of the accused. Finding a group of respected and qualified people who can be seen as acceptable to both sides will be difficult. Although one possibility may be to use jurors from respected neutral countries, those distinguished enough for the international community to accept their judgment would be unlikely to accept an appointment to the bench that would endanger their neutral status.

Once again, France emerges as a prime candidate. Though far from neutral, it's stance against the United States during Operation Iraqi Freedom gives it a modicum of legitimacy in the eyes of the Arab nations and promotes the appearance of impartiality internationally. Additionally, the French government's quest to become a greater international power lessens the possibility of refusal. Accordingly, France should be requested to provide the Chief Justice. The other countries included in the pre-trial conference should be asked to provide justices, with the United Nations and Iraqi representatives serving as non-voting members of the judiciary. The combination of nations ensures one Muslim judge (Albania), two former Soviet Block countries (Poland and Albania), one country opposed to the invasion of Iraq (France) and the three primary members of the coalition (US, UK, and Australia). With the UN representative providing an international perspective and Iraqi representative providing local insights, the court should be receive positive internationally perception.

Selection of Counsel

From the countries selected to participate in a pre-trial conference will be an additional requirement for competent, highly respected prosecutors and defenders. One major criticism of Tokyo was the lack of experience in international law at all levels of the trial. In fact, Justice Pal was the only person with significant experience in the subject. Most others were political appointees of their country detailed to the process. Nuremberg presented another option. The four countries heading the trials sent some of their most experienced and esteemed prosecutors like United States Supreme Court Justice Robert Jackson, and British Attorney General Sir Hartley Shawcross to prosecute the trial. Although the level of experience in international law has increased since the 1940s, the potential for getting such august figures such as a British Attorney General and a Supreme Court Justice may have decreased. While they would provide a phenomenal opportunity to add to the legitimacy of the trial, political reality internal to many prosecuting nations could render the option unsustainable. For example, the removal of one of the nine members of the United States Supreme Court could have an effect on its rulings that could have enduring political ramifications within the country. However, enough respected members of the legal community exist to find acceptable replacements.

Invitees to the pretrial conference must give additional consideration to the possibility of Iraqi representation on the court. Years after the Tokyo trial, Justice Röling revealed his conviction that there should have been Japanese representation on the bench—a belief echoed by Justice Pal. If Iraqis are included in the planning conferences, *Sharia* law is taken into account in the prosecution and defense, and the coalition insists the *Ba'ath* regime—not the Iraqi people— are responsibility for the atrocities of the past few decades, it would be a difficult stretch to exclude Iraqi representation in the prosecution and judges. Again, international perception is key to the decision.

International perception also dictates that military prosecutors and justices should be relegated to supporting roles. Iraqi trials could be held as a military tribunal but, in reality, fall into the Clausewitzian perspective in which politics take the lead of military affairs. Although war crimes are included in the trinity of crimes under international law, the trial must focus on the other two accusations—crimes against peace and crimes against humanity—to further the image the Coalition desires to put forth.[75] Military prosecutors and justices will muddle message the Coalition is attempting to forward to the world. Simply stated, the trial is not about wartime conduct. It must be an effort to convey to the world the immensity of the atrocities committed by a morally bankrupt regime headed by Saddam Hussein.

Selection of Defendants

Before a trial can be held, there must be a prisoner's dock, presumably filled with prisoners. The necessity drives the next question: who should be tried? Nuremberg and Tokyo both offer insight into answering the question. The most important lesson learned in Tokyo was try the leader. Removal of the Japanese emperor from the dock was possibly the greatest impediment to a unified front of the Justices and positive perception of justice by the public. Forwarding to the 21st century, it is almost universally understood and agreed upon that at a minimum, Saddam Hussein must be tried. An important lesson of the Nuremberg trials was to judge the movement. During the Nuremberg Trials, the Nazi party itself was tried and found guilty of war crimes. The guilty verdict criminalized the movement and furthered the delegitimization of the former regime. Including the Ba'ath party in the list of defendants could have the same effect in Iraq.

Furthering the question of the docket, the now famous decks of cards issued to Coalition Troops, containing a different "bad guy" on each card, make an inherent accusation that must be addressed. Every person portrayed on the deck of fifty-two, even if he has been released, must be tried. Since the United States publicly depicted these people as the source of many crimes in Iraq, they must be given the opportunity to exonerate themselves. Although some may be shown

---

[75] The three charges; crimes against humanity, crimes against peace, and war crimes were contentious in the Nuremberg and Tokyo trial. Originally billed as *post facto* law legislated from the bench, the charges have been codified into international law and a precedent has been set at the two trials and subsequent attempts such as the ICTY and ICTR.

to be other than guilty, a verdict of "innocent" or "not guilty" only enhances the status of the Coalition and the court by depicting their fairness. As of December 13, 2003, forty-one of the original fifty-two people depicted on the cards had been captured or killed.[76]

For additional defendants, one might be tempted to look to the Iraqis themselves to recommend who should be tried. Since such a course of action could bring an untenable amount of accused personnel, local courts would have to be established to deal with overflow. Yet Iraqi law currently differs significantly from international law, courts are poorly established, ethnic and racial tensions are extreme, and those on the court are barely trusted. It would seem that local trials could bring with them a bevy of potential problems that would have to be considered and could be a "bridge too far." Once again, the Nuremberg trials hold a lesson for the modern day.

Post WWII trials in Germany were held according to a tiered system with only the worst (and most visible) offenders remanded to the Nuremberg trials.[77] The rest were sent to regional and local courts created to deal with various categories of offenders, supervised by the Allies. The procedure was mirrored in Japan. A similar tiered system in Iraq could help the return of the rule of law by empowering and therefore reenergizing faith in the local judiciary while simultaneously vetting the judges for a future role in Iraqi government. Those determined to be the greatest offenders (currently the individuals depicted on the playing cards) would be sent to Paris for an international trial. A second and third tier could be tried at the national and local level administered by Iraqi judges under the supervision of Coalition or UN sponsored supervisors, with security provided by the Coalition. Use of Coalition or UN supervisors would facilitate the vetting process, while Coalition security personnel would ensure a safe venue free of Ba'athist aggression or pressure. Trial of at least some of the offenders (especially those known

---

[76] Gary Miller. *Congressman Gary Miller, 42d Congressional District News, December 14th, 2003*. Online at http://www.house.gov/garymiller/DeckofCards html. Accessed 18 February, 2004. Internet.

by residents) at the local level would serve to make the results more tangible to Iraqis. Again, use of UN sponsored advisors could help to polish the tarnished perception of the legal appendages of the UN while drawing the UN closer to the Coalition and insinuating it into the Iraqi reconstruction.

A Just Outcome?

A trial of the former leaders of Iraq will be one of the most watched, discussed, criticized and maligned events of the decade. No matter how careful law is applied, what processes are used, who is included in the trial, bench, and prosecution, or what outcome is reached, international dissonance will resound. The best case for which organizers of the trial can hope is to achieve a desired set of goals that will help to frame a just outcome. President Bush's goal of withstanding international scrutiny offers insight into one very real concern that must be addressed when contemplating a just outcome. Likewise, Robert Jackson's conviction, voiced over fifty years ago, that the goal of the Nuremberg trial was to promote international law still has validity in modern times. It would be easy to state that a just outcome will depend on the eye of the beholder, but not true. An outcome will only be reckoned as just if it satisfies the perception of three patrons: international, Iraqi, and internal.

First, the preponderance of the international community must be convinced that justice has been equitably served under international law. Both Justice Jackson and President Bush address the necessity from opposite, yet intertwined ends. If the ruling of the court does not withstand international scrutiny, there will be no chance to advance the cause of international law. Without advancing the cause of international law and portraying the court as an attempt to right a

---

[77] ECLIPSE, Memorandum #19.

wrong, the United States will lose international prestige and find increasing international pressure in all undertakings—including future advancement of international law.

International opinion is very closely linked to the opinion of the Iraqi people. Trial and conviction of the former *Ba'ath* party officials will be the keystone of the return of law to Iraq. The message sent in its verdict will either encourage the Iraqi people to believe the Coalition understands the needs of the people and is ready to meet them, or that the Coalition is merely bent on revenge and will leave as soon as the desire is fulfilled. An innate requirement of justice— understanding the local beliefs, norms, and customs—is essential to a verdict that meets the requirements of justice for the Iraqi people and furthers the Coalition message: "we are here to help."

The final requirement is indigenous to each member state of the coalition. Internally to each country is the reality that the war in Iraq was a political decision with potential political repercussions if the desired endstate is not reached. Therefore, satisfying each political leader's constituency is of indisputable concern. Failure to meet the goals imbued in the political rhetoric forwarded as reason for war undermines the administration of each nation and, in the case of less firmly established governments, could threaten a nationwide crisis of confidence and a toppling of the government.

One cornerstone of *Jus in Bello* is the notion that the severity of punishment must be consistent with the seriousness of the crime. An enigma contained within the construct is the concept of "severe punishment." The ancient code of "an eye for an eye, a tooth for a tooth" is actively practiced in many Middle Eastern nations yet often shunned in the West. Accordingly, application of the death penalty may prove to be the most divisive part of the trial. If convicted, should Saddam Hussein receive the death penalty? International and *Sharia* law as well as historical precedent all allow for the provision, but is it the best choice? Perhaps not.

Although the death sentence gives final closure to the evils perpetrated by Saddam Hussein and his cronies, it may have unfortunate side effects. His execution could be used by other factions, such as *Al Qaeda* to vilify the United States and elevate Hussein to the status of martyr while exacerbating philosophical rifts within the nation over the death penalty. Conversely, a life sentence of imprisonment may serve to achieve the desired result. Reducing the formerly feared leaders of the regime to the status of common criminal and giving the world a tangible, lasting, and living symbol of evil prevents their deification and may serve as a substantial representation of the fairness and greatness of American justice.

Conclusion

Ultimately, whether the stated purpose of the trials is to achieve a better peace, withstand international scrutiny, right a wrong, or simply see justice done, the fact remains that the real intent of the trial will be to promote the image of the United States as the champion of peace. The verdict of the trial is almost inconsequential. The true measure of the success of the trial will the acceptance of the trial itself. Both Tokyo and Nuremberg present historical case studies that offer insight into the trial of the future. From the sober, deliberate events that characterized Nuremberg to the spurious affectation that was Tokyo, creators of the trial against the former leaders in Iraq can find clues into its successful application. Though not exactly modeled like its precursors, the upcoming trial will find its character somewhere in the middle.

APPENDIX 1. London Agreement of August 8th 1945[78]

AGREEMENT by the Government of the UNITED STATES OF AMERICA, the Provisional Government of the FRENCH REPUBLIC, the Government of the UNITED KINGDOM OF GREAT BRITAIN AND NORTHERN IRELAND and the Government of the UNION OF SOVIET SOCIALIST REPUBLICS for the Prosecution and Punishment of the MAJOR WAR CRIMINALS of the EUROPEAN AXIS

WHEREAS the United Nations have from time to time made declarations of their intention that War Criminals shall be brought to justice;

AND WHEREAS the Moscow Declaration of the 30th October 1943 on German atrocities in Occupied Europe stated that those German Officers and men and members of the Nazi Party who have been responsible for or have taken a consenting part in atrocities and crimes will be sent back to the countries in which their abominable deeds were done in order that they may be judged and punished according to the laws of these liberated countries and of the free Governments that will be created therein;

AND WHEREAS this Declaration was stated to be without prejudice to the case of major criminals whose offenses have no particular geographical location and who will be punished by the joint decision of the Governments of the Allies;

NOW THEREFORE the Government of the United States of America, the Provisional Government of the French Republic, the Government of the United Kingdom of Great Britain and Northern Ireland and the Government of the Union of Soviet Socialist Republics (hereinafter called "the Signatories") acting in the interests of all the United Nations and by their representatives duly authorized thereto have concluded this Agreement.

Article 1. There shall be established after consultation with the Control Council for Germany an International Military Tribunal for the trial of war criminals whose offenses have no particular geographical location whether they be accused individually or in their capacity as members of the organizations or groups or in both capacities.

Article 2. The constitution, jurisdiction and functions of the International Military Tribunal shall be those set in the Charter annexed to this Agreement, which Charter shall form an integral part of this Agreement.

Article 3. Each of the Signatories shall take the necessary steps to make available for the investigation of the charges and trial the major war criminals detained by them who are to be tried by the International Military Tribunal. The Signatories shall also use their best endeavors to make available for investigation of the charges against and the trial before the International Military Tribunal such of the major war criminals as are not in the territories of any of the Signatories.

Article 4. Nothing in this Agreement shall prejudice the provisions established by the Moscow Declaration concerning the return of war criminals to the countries where they committed their crimes.

Article 5. Any Government of the United Nations may adhere to this Agreement by notice given through the diplomatic channel to the Government of the United Kingdom, who shall inform the other signatory and adhering Governments of each such adherence.

Article 6. Nothing in this Agreement shall prejudice the jurisdiction or the powers of any national or occupation court established or to be established in any allied territory or in Germany for the trial of war criminals.

---

[78] This document along with the entire record of the Nuremberg trials can be found online at the Avalon Project at Yale law school. The URL for this specific document is http://www.yale.edu/lawweb/avalon/imt/proc/imtchart htm.

Article 7. This Agreement shall come into force on the day of signature and shall remain in force for the period of one year and shall continue thereafter, subject to the right of any Signatory to give, through the diplomatic channel, one month's notice of intention to terminate it. Such termination shall not prejudice any proceedings already taken or any findings already made in pursuance of this Agreement.

IN WITNESS WHEREOF the Undersigned have signed the present Agreement.

DONE in quadruplicate in London this 8th day of August 1945 each in English, French and Russian, and each text to have equal authenticity.

For the Government of the United States of America
Robert H. Jackson
For the Provisional Government of the French Republic
Robert Falco
For the Government of the United Kingdom of Great Britain and Northern Ireland
Jowitt C.
For the Government of the Union of Soviet Socialist Republics
I. Nikitchenko
A. Trainin

APPENDIX 2. Articles of the Kellog-Briand Pact[79]

ARTICLE I

The High Contracting Parties solemnly declare in the names of their respective peoples that they condemn recourse to war for the solution of international controversies, and renounce it, as an instrument of national policy in their relations with one another.

ARTICLE II

The High Contracting Parties agree that the settlement or solution of all disputes or conflicts of whatever nature or of whatever origin they may be, which may arise among them, shall never be sought except by pacific means.

ARTICLE III

The present Treaty shall be ratified by the High Contracting Parties named in the Preamble in accordance with their respective constitutional requirements, and shall take effect as between them as soon as all their several instruments of ratification shall have been deposited at Washington.

This Treaty shall, when it has come into effect as prescribed in the preceding paragraph, remain open as long as may be necessary for adherence by all the other Powers of the world. Every instrument evidencing the adherence of a Power shall be deposited at Washington and the Treaty shall immediately upon such deposit become effective as; between the Power thus adhering and the other Powers parties hereto.

It shall be the duty of the Government of the United States to furnish each Government named in the Preamble and every Government subsequently adhering to this Treaty with a certified copy of the Treaty and of every instrument of ratification or adherence. It shall also be the duty of the Government of the United States telegraphically to notify such Governments immediately upon the deposit with it of each instrument of ratification or adherence.

IN FAITH WHEREOF the respective Plenipotentiaries have signed this Treaty in the French and English languages both texts having equal force, and hereunto affix their seals.

DONE at Paris, the twenty seventh day of August in the year one thousand nine hundred and twenty-eight.

---

[79]Yale University, Avalon Project. http://www.yale.edu/lawweb/avalon/imt/proc/imtconst htm.

APPENDIX 3. Article 6, Constitution of the International Military Tribunal[80]

The Tribunal established by the Agreement referred to m Article 1 hereof for the trial and punishment of the major war criminals of the European Axis countries shall have the power to try and punish persons who, acting in the interests of the European Axis countries, whether as individuals or as members of organizations, committed any of the following crimes.

The following acts, or any of them, are crimes coming within the jurisdiction of the Tribunal for which there shall be individual responsibility:

CRIMES AGAINST PEACE: namely, planning, preparation, initiation or waging of a war of aggression, or a war in violation of international treaties, agreements or assurances, or participation in a common plan or conspiracy for the accomplishment of any of the foregoing;

WAR CRIMES: namely, violations of the laws or customs of war. Such violations shall include, but not be limited to, murder, ill-treatment or deportation to slave labor or for any other purpose of civilian population of or in occupied territory, murder or ill-treatment of prisoners of war or persons on the seas, killing of hostages, plunder of public or private property, wanton destruction of cities, towns or villages, or devastation not justified by military necessity;

CRIMES AGAINST HUMANITY: namely, murder, extermination, enslavement, deportation, and other inhumane acts committed against any civilian population, before or during the war; or persecutions on political, racial or religious grounds in execution of or in connection with any crime within the jurisdiction of the Tribunal, whether or not in violation of the domestic law of the country where perpetrated.

Leaders, organizers, instigators and accomplices participating in the formulation or execution of a common plan or conspiracy to commit any of the foregoing crimes are responsible for all acts performed by any persons in execution of such plan.

---

[80] Yale University, Avalon Project. http://www.yale.edu/lawweb/avalon/imt/proc/imtconst htm.

APPENDIX 4. ANNEX 2, Section 3 (b) of the Potsdam Declaration Proclamation Defining Terms for Japanese Surrender, July 26, 1945[81]

(1) We-The President of the United States, the President of the National Government of the Republic of China, and the Prime Minister of Great Britain, representing the hundreds of millions of our countrymen, have conferred and agree that Japan shall be given an opportunity to end this war.

(2) The prodigious land, sea and air forces of the United States, the British Empire and of China, many times reinforced by their armies and air fleets from the west, are poised to strike the final blows upon Japan. This military power is sustained and inspired by the determination of all the Allied Nations to prosecute the war against Japan until she ceases to resist.

(3) The result of the futile and senseless German resistance to the might of the aroused free peoples of the world stands forth in awful clarity as an example to the people of Japan. The might that now converges on Japan is immeasurably greater than that which, when applied to the resisting Nazis, necessarily laid waste to the lands, the industry and the method of life of the whole German people. The full application of our military power, backed by our resolve, All mean the inevitable and complete destruction of the Japanese armed forces and just as inevitably the utter devastation of the Japanese homeland.

(4) The time has come for Japan to decide whether she will continue to be controlled by those self-willed militaristic advisers whose unintelligent calculations have brought the Empire of Japan to the threshold of annihilation, or whether she will follow the path of reason.

(5) Following are our terms. We will not deviate from them. There are no alternatives. We shall brook no delay.

(6) There must be eliminated for all time the authority and influence of those who have deceived and misled the people of Japan into embarking on world conquest, for we insist that a new order of peace security and justice will be impossible until irresponsible militarism is driven from the world.

(7) Until such a new order is established and until there is convincing proof that Japan's war-making power is destroyed, points in Japanese territory to be designated by the Allies shall be occupied to secure the achievement of the basic objectives we are here setting forth.

(8) The terms of the Cairo Declaration shall be carried out and Japanese sovereignty shall be limited to the islands of Honshu, Hokkaido, Kyushu, Shikoku and such minor islands as we determine.

(9) The Japanese military forces, after being completely disarmed, shall be permitted to return to their homes with the opportunity to lead peaceful and productive lives.

(10) We do not intend that the Japanese shall be enslaved as a race or destroyed as a nation, but stern justice shall be meted out to all war criminals, including those who have visited cruelties upon our prisoners. The Japanese Government shall remove all obstacles to the revival and strengthening of democratic tendencies among the Japanese people. Freedom of speech, of religion, and of thought, as well as respect for the fundamental human rights shall be established.

(11) Japan shall be permitted to maintain such industries as will sustain her economy and permit the exaction of just reparations in kind, but not those [industries] which would enable her

---

[81] Website of the Harry S. Truman Library. [website online] http://www.trumanlibrary.org/ whistlestop/study_collections/bomb/large/ferrell_book/ferrell_book_chap7.htm.

to re-arm for war. To this end, access to, as distinguished from control of, raw materials shall be permitted. Eventual Japanese participation in world trade relations shall be permitted.

(12) The occupying forces of the Allies shall be withdrawn from Japan as soon as these objectives have been accomplished and there has been established in accordance with the freely expressed will of the Japanese people a peacefully inclined and responsible government.

(13) We call upon the government of Japan to proclaim now the unconditional surrender of all Japanese armed forces, and to provide proper and adequate assurances of their good faith in such action. The alternative for Japan is prompt and utter destruction.

APPENDIX 5. Draft Declaration on Rights and Duties of States[82]

-Whereas the States of the world form a community governed by international law,

-Whereas the progressive development of international law requires effective organization of the community of States,

-Whereas a great majority of the States of the world have accordingly established a new international order under the Charter of the United Nations, and most of the other States of the world have declared their desire to live within this order,

-Whereas a primary purpose of the United Nations is to maintain international peace and security, and the reign of law and justice is essential to the realization of this purpose, and

-Whereas it is therefore desirable to formulate certain basic rights and duties of States in the light of new developments of international law and in harmony with the Charter of the United Nations,

-The General Assembly of the United Nations adopts and proclaims this Declaration on Rights and Duties of States:

Article 1   Every State has the right to independence and hence to exercise freely, without dictation by any other State, all its legal powers, including the choice of its own form of government.

Article 2   Every State has the right to exercise jurisdiction over its territory and over all persons and things therein, subject to the immunities recognized by international law.

Article 3   Every State has the duty to refrain from intervention in the internal or external affairs of any other State.

Article 4   Every State has the duty to refrain from fomenting civil strife in the territory of another State, and to prevent the organization within its territory of activities calculated to foment such civil strife.

Article 5   Every State has the right to equality in law with every other State.

Article 6   Every State has the duty to treat all persons under its jurisdiction with respect for human rights and fundamental freedoms, without distinction as to race, sex, language, or religion.

Article 7   Every State has the duty to ensure that conditions prevailing in its territory do not menace international peace and order.

Article 8   Every State has the duty to settle its disputes with other States by peaceful means in such a manner that international peace and security, and justice, are not endangered.

Article 9   Every State has the duty to refrain from resorting to war as an instrument of national policy, and to refrain from the threat or use of force against the territorial integrity or political independence of another State in any other manner inconsistent with international law and order.

Article 10   Every State has the duty to refrain from giving assistance to any State which is acting in violation of article 9, or against which the United Nations is taking preventive or enforcement action.

Article 11   Every State has the duty to refrain from recognizing any territorial acquisition by another State acting in violation of article 9.

Article 12   Every State has the right of individual or collective self-defence against armed attack.

Article 13   Every State has the duty to carry out in good faith its obligations arising from

---

[82] ILC. http://www.un.org/law/ilc/texts/decfra.htm.

treaties and other sources of international law, and it may not invoke provisions in its constitution or its laws as an excuse for failure to perform this duty.

Article 14 Every State has the duty to conduct its relations with other States in accordance with international law and with the principle that the sovereignty of each State is subject to the supremacy of international law.

BIBLIOGRAPHY

Books

Annan, Noel. *Changing Enemies*. New York: W. W, Norton & Company, 1996.

Armstrong, Karen. *Islam, A Short History*. New York: Random House, 2000.

Berman, Paul. *Terror and Liberalism*. New York: W. W. Norton & Company, 2003.

Bix, Herbert P. *Hirohito and the Making of Modern Japan*. New York: Harper Collins Publishers, 2000.

Dobbins, James, et al. *America's Role in Nation Building: From Germany to Iraq*. Santa Monica, California: RAND, 2003.

Dower, John W. *Embracing Defeat: Japan in the Wake of World War II*. New York: W.W. Norton/ New Press, 1999.

Esposito, John L. *The Islamic Threat Myth or Reality? Third Edition*. New York: Oxford University Press, Inc, 1999.

Ginn John L. *Sugamo Prison, Tokyo, An Account of the Trial and Sentencing of Japanese War Criminals in 1948 by a U. S. Participant*. Jefferson, North Carolina: McFarland & Company, 1992.

Gimbal, John. *The Origins of the Marshall Plan*. Stanford California: Stanford University Press, 1976.

Hayes, Grace P. *History of the Joint Chiefs of Staff in WWII, The War Against Japan*. Annapolis, Maryland: Naval Institute Press, 1982.

Hoffer, Eric. *The True Believer, Thoughts on the Nature of Mass Movements*. New York: Harper and Row, 1966.

Hoffman, Bruce. *Inside Terrorism*. New York: Columbia University Press, 1998.

Hogan, Michael J. *The Marshall Plan: America, Britain, and the reconstruction of Western Europe, 1947-1952*. New York: Cambridge University Press, 1987.

Huntington, Samuel P. *The Clash of Civilizations and the Remaking of World Order*. New York: Simon and Schuster, 1996.

Jurgensmeyer, Mark. *Terror in the Mind of God, The Global Rise of Religious Violence*. Berkeley California: University of California Press, 2001.

Kaplan, Robert D. *The Coming Anarchy: Shattering the Dreams of the Post Cold War*. New York: Random House, 2000.

Liddel-Hart Basil H., *Strategy*, New York: Signet, 1974.

Lewis, Bernard. *What Went Wrong? Western Impact and Middle East Response*. Oxford: Oxford University Press, 2002.

Manchester, William. *American Caesar: Douglas MacArthur 1880-1964*. New York: Bantam Books, 1996.

Marrus, Michael R. *The Nuremberg War Crimes Trial, 1945-46; A Documentary History*. Boston: Bedford Books, 1997.

Minear, Richard, *Victors' Justice: The Tokyo War Crimes Trial.* Princeton, New Jersey: Princeton University Press, 1973.

O'Neill, Bard. *Insurgency & Terrorism: Inside Modern Revolutionary Warfare.* Washington D.C.: Brassey's Inc, 2001.

Pollack, Kenneth M. *Arabs At War; Military Effectiveness 1948-1991.* Lincoln, Nebraska: University of Nebraska Press, 2002.

Schaller, Michael. *The American Occupation of Japan: The Origins of the Cold War in Asia.* Oxford: Oxford University Press, 1997.

Schonberger, Howard B. *Aftermath of War: Americans and the Remaking of Japan, 1945-1952.* Kent, Ohio: Kent State University Press, 1989.

Sigal, Leon B. *Fighting to a Finish: The Politics of War Termination in the United States and Japan, 1945.* Ithaca, New York: Cornell University Press, 1989

Skates, John R. *The Invasion of Japan: Alternative to the Bomb.* Columbia, South Carolina: University of South Carolina Press, 2000.

Smith, Arthur Lee. *The War for the German Mind: Re-educating Hitler's Soldiers.* Providence, Rhode Island: Berghahn Books, 1996.

Snell, John L. *Wartime Origins of the East West Dilemma Over Germany.* New Orleans, Louisiana: The Hauser Press, 1958.

Taylor, Telford. *The Anatomy of the Nuremberg Trials; A Personal Memoir.* New York: Alford A. Knopf, 1992.

_____ *Nuremberg and Vietnam: An American Tragedy.* Chicago: Quadrangle Books, 1970.

Tent, James F. *Mission on the Rhine: Reeducation and "Denazification" In American-Occupied Germany.* Chicago: University of Chicago Press, 1982.

United Nations War Crimes Commission. *Law Reports of Trials of War Criminals. Selected and Prepared by the United Nations War Crimes Commission.* Volume IV. London: HMSO, 1948. [online] http://www.ess.uwe.ac.uk/genocide/trials.htm. Accessed 15 April, 2004.

Weinberg, Gerhard L. *A World at Arms : A Global History of World War II.* Oxford: Cambridge University Press, 1995.

Wilson, Theodore A. *The Marshall Plan, 1947-1951.* New York: Foreign Policy Association, 1977.

Journals and Periodicals

Allen, Lafe F. "Education Reform in Japan", *The Yale Review* 36, June 1947, 705-716.

Bix, Herbert P. "The Showa Emperor's Monologue and the Problem of War Responsibility." *Journal of Japanese Studies* 18:2, 1992.

Dobbins, James. "Nation Building: The Inescapable Responsibility of the World's Only Superpower." *Rand Review*, Vol. 27, No. 2 (Summer 2003). [online] http://www.rand. org/publications/ randreview/issues/summer2003/nation1.html. Accessed 18 January, 2003.

Dower, John. "Occupation Preoccupation" *New York Times*, March 30, 2003. [online] http://www.nytimes.com/2003/03/30/magazine/30QUESTIONS.html?ex=1074574800&en=635ca77f06e4ba48&ei=5070. Accessed 18 January, 2004.

Dower, John. "Is the U.S. Repeating the Mistakes of Japan in the 1930s?." *History News Network*, June 30, 2003. [online] http://hnn.us/articles/1534.html Accessed 18 January, 2004.

Dower John. "Bush's Comparison of Iraq with Postwar Japan Ignores the Facts." *Los Angeles Times*, December 8, 2003.

Hoffman, Bruce. "Old Madness, New Methods, Revival of Religious Terrorism Begs for Broader U.S. Policy." *Rand Review* [journal online] http://www.rand.org/publications/randreview/ issues/ rr.winter98.9/methods.html. Accessed 21 September, 2003.

Hille, Henry L. "Eighth Army's Role in the Military Government of Japan", *Military Review*, 27: 9-18 February 1948.

Jansen, Marius B. "Education and Politics in Japan", *Foreign Affairs* 36, July 1957.

Manwaring, Max G. "Toward an Understanding of Insurgency Wars: The Paradigm." In Max G. Manwaring, ed. *Uncomfortable Wars: Toward a New Paradigm of Low Intensity Conflict*. (Bolder, CO: Westview Press, 1991) Chapter 2.

Shills, Edward. "The Concept and Function of Ideology." *International Encyclopedia of the Social Sciences. Volume 7.* New York: The Macmillan Company and the Free Press, 1972, 66-76.

Spiller, Roger J. "Cherry Blossoms Falling: Japanese Combat Behavior at War's End." 1945: *War and Peace in the Pacific: Selected Essays.* Peter Dennis, ed. Canberra, Australia: The Australian War Memorial, 1999, 1-21.

Spiro, Herbert J. "Totalitarianism." *International Encyclopedia of the Social Sciences. Volume 15.* New York: The Macmillan Company and the Free Press, 1972, 106-112.

Snell, John. "Wartime Origins of the East-West Dilemma Over Germany." *American Historical Review*, Vol. 65, No. 2, Jan, 1960, 342-343.

Switzer, John S. "Military Government in Japan", *Military Review*, 34: 23-25 April 1954.

Wallace, Anthony F. C. "Mass Phenomena." *International Encyclopedia of the Social Sciences. Volume 9.* New York: The Macmillan Company and the Free Press, 1972, 54-57.

Wiktorowicz, Quintan. "The New Global Threat: Transnational Salafis and Jihad." *Middle East Policy.* Vol VIII, No. 4, December 2001, 18-38.

United States Government Publications

Commander in Chief, US Pacific Fleet and Pacific Oceans Area. *Report of Surrender and Occupation of Japan*, 11 February 1946.

General Headquarters, Southwest Pacific. *Basic Outline Plan for "BLACKLIST" Operations to Occupy Japan Proper and Korea After Surrender or Collapse*, General HQ, Southwest Pacific, 1945.

General HQ, Southwest Pacific. *Staff Study, Operation BAKER-SIXTY (Occupation of Tokyo).* GHQ, Southwest Pacific, 1945.

Hudson, Walter M. *The U.S. Military Government and Democratic Reform and "Denazification" In Bavaria, 1945-47.* Fort Leavenworth, Kansas: U.S. Army Command and General Staff College, 1997.

International Military Tribunal. *Control Council Law No. 10; Punishment Of Persons Guilty Of War Crimes, Crimes Against Peace And Against Humanity*. 20 December 1945. [online] http://www.yale.edu/ lawweb/avalon/imt/imt10.htm. Accessed 1 March, 2004.

Joint Chiefs of Staff. *Directive on the Identification and Apprehension of Persons Suspected of War Crimes or Other Offenses and Trial of Certain* [online] http://www.yale.edu/ lawweb/avalon/imt/imtjcs.htm. Accessed 1 March, 2004.

_____. *Doctrine for Joint Operations, Joint Publication 3-0.* Washington D.C.: U.S. JCS, 10 September, 2001.

_____. *Doctrine for Joint Psychological Operations, Joint Publication 3-53.* Washington D.C.: U.S. JCS, 10 July, 1996.

_____. *Doctrine for Planning Joint Operations, Joint Publication 5.0.* Washington D.C.: U.S. JCS, 13 April, 1995

_____. *Joint Doctrine for Civil Affairs, Joint Publication 3-57.1.* Washington D.C.: U.S. JCS, 14 April, 2003.

_____. *Joint Doctrine for Civil Military Operations, Joint Publication 3-57.* Washington D.C.: U.S. JCS, 8 February, 2001.

_____. *Joint Doctrine for Military Operations Other Than War, Joint Publication 3-07.* Washington D.C.: U.S. JCS, 16 June, 1995.

_____. *Tactics Techniques and Procedures for Antiterrorism, Joint Publication 3-07.2.* Washington D.C.: U.S. JCS, 17 March, 1998.

_____. *Tactics Techniques and Procedures for Foreign Internal Defense (FID), Joint Publication 3-07.1.* Washington D.C.: U.S. JCS, 26 June, 1996

_____. *Tactics Techniques and Procedures for Peace Operations, Joint Publication 3-07.3.* Washington D.C.: U.S. JCS, 12 February, 1999.

Korman, John G. *U. S. "Denazification" Policy in Germany, 1944-1950.* Bad Godesberg-Mehlheim, Germany: Office of the Executive Secretary, Office of the U. S. High Commissioner for Germany, 1952.

Office Of U.S. Chief Of Counsel. *General Memorandum No. 15; Organization for Subsequent Proceedings.* March 20, 1946. [online] http://www.yale.edu/lawweb/avalon/ imt/imt10.htm. Accessed 1 March, 2004.

SCAP Monograph No. 5 Trials of Class "B" and "C" War Criminals. Washington: Department of the Army. The Adjutant General's Office. Department of Records Branch. 1951.

Supreme Commander for the Allied Powers. *Summation of Non-Military Activities in Japan and Korea*, General HQ, SCAP, Sept 1945 to June 1945, Seven Volumes.

Supreme HQ, Allied Expeditionary Force. *Operation Eclipse, Appreciation and Outline Plan.* SHAEF, 10 November 1944.

The General Board, United States Forces, European Theater. *Procedures Followed by Civil Affairs and Military Government in the Restoration, Reorganization, and Supervision of Indigenous Civil Administration.* SHAEF, 17 June, 1945.

U. S. Army Civic Affairs School. *Planning for the Occupation of Germany, Special Text 41-10-62*, U. S. Army Civic Affairs School, 1947.

U.S. Army Civil Affairs School *Handbook for Military Government in Germany, Special Text 41-10-60*, U.S. Army Civil Affairs School. 1943.

U.S. Department of State. *The United States and Germany, 1945-1955.* Department of State Publication 5827. United States Government Printing Office: May, 1955.

United States Army Civil Affairs School. *American Military Government Courts in Germany, With Special Reference to Historic Practice and Their Role in the Democratization of the German People, Special Text 41-10-2.* U.S. Army Civil Affairs School, 1953.

US Army Forces Pacific. *Tentative Troop List by Type Units for "BLACKLIST".* Operations, General HQ, US Army Forces Pacific, 8 August 1945.

War Department. *FM 27-5, US Army and Navy Manual of Military Government and Civil Affairs. (OPNAV 50E-3).* U.S. Government, 22 Dec 1943.

War Department. *US Initial Post-Surrender Policy for Japan.* 22 September 1945.

Theses Studies and Other Papers

Barton, Frederick D. and Bathsheba N. Crocker. "A Wiser Peace: An Action Strategy for a Post Conflict Iraq." Washington DC: Center for Strategic and International Studies. January, 2003. [online] http://www.csis.org/isp/wiserpeace.pdf. Accessed 3 December, 2003.

Barton, Frederick D. and Bathsheba N. Crocker. "Post Conflict Reconstruction." Washington, DC: Center for Strategic and International Studies: 2001. [online] http://www.csis.org/isp/pcr/framework.pdf. Accessed 3 December, 2003.

Bush, George. "President Discusses the Future of Iraq." Speech to the American Enterprise Institute, 26 February, 2003. [online] http://www.whitehouse.gov/news/releases/2003/02/ 20030226-11.html. Accessed 1 March, 2004.

Bush, George. Press Conference, 15 December, 2003. Online at http://www.whitehouse.gov/news/releases/2003/12/20031215-3.html. Accessed 1 March, 2004.

Forman, Johana Mendelson. "Achieving Socio-Economic Well-Being in Post-Conflict Settings." Post Conflict Reconstruction Project, Center for Strategic and International Studies: June 9, 2002. [online] http://www.csis.org/isp/pcr/socioeconomicpaper.pdf. Accessed 1 March, 2004.

Fournoy, Michele. "Interagency Strategy and Planning for Post-Conflict Reconstruction." Post Conflict Reconstruction Project. Center for Strategic and International Studies: March 27, 2002. [online] http://www.csis.org/isp/pcr/strategy.pdf. Accessed 3 December, 2003, Internet.

Fournoy, Michele and Pan, Michael. "Justice and Reconciliation" Post Conflict Reconstruction Project, Center for Strategic and International Studies. [online] http://www.csis.org/isp/pcr/justicepaper.pdf. Accessed 3 December, 2003.

Hoffman, Bruce and Jennifer Morrison Taw. *A Strategic Framework for Countering Terrorism and Insurgency.* Santa Monica, California: RAND, 1992.

Hoffman, Bruce. *Terrorist Targeting: Tactics, Trends and Potentialities.* Santa Monica, California: RAND, 1992.

International Military Tribunal. "Second Day, Wednesday, 11/21/1945, Part 04", in Trial of the Major War Criminals before the International Military Tribunal. Volume II. Proceedings: 11/14/1945-11/30/1945. [Official text in the English language.] Nuremberg: IMT, 1947. pp. 98-102. Online at http://www.courttv.com/archive/casefiles/nuremberg/jackson.html. Accessed 18 January, 2004.

Jennings. Ray Salvatore. "The Road Ahead: Lessons in Nation Building from Japan, Germany, and Afghanistan for Postwar Iraq," *United States Institute of Peace Peaceworks #49* (7 May, 2003). [journal online] http://www.usip.org/pubs/peaceworks/ pwks49.html. Accessed 3 March, 2004.

Lipton, Leon. *Study of Policy Guidance Provided for U. S. Military Governance in Germany WWII (Parts I and II)*. Government Affairs Institute. Washington D. C. March, 1960.

McCreedy, Kenneth O. "Planning the Peace: Operation ECLIPSE and the Occupation of Germany." Fort Leavenworth, Kansas: School for Advanced Military Studies, U.S. Army Command and General Staff College, 1995.

Montgomery, John D. *The Purge in Occupied Japan*. Project Legate TM ORO-Y-48(FEC), Johns Hopkins University Operations Research Office for the Department of the Army: Chevy Chase MD, 3 July, 1953.

Oglobin, Peter. *The Purge in Occupied Japan, Appendix I: The Role of SCAP Intelligence Agencies in the Purge of Japanese Undesirables*. Project Legate TM ORO-Y-48(FEC), Johns Hopkins University Operations Research Office for the Department of the Army: Chevy Chase MD, 18 January, 1954.

Orr, Robert. "Meeting the Challenges of Governance and Participation in Post-Conflict Settings." Post Conflict Reconstruction Project, Center for Strategic and International Studies, July 8, 2002. [online] http://www.csis.org/isp/pcr/governancepaper.pdf. Accessed 3 December, 2003.

Pei Minxin and Sara Kasper. "Lessons from the Past: The American Record in Nation-Building." *Website of the Carnegie Endowment for International Peace*. [article online] http://www.ceip.org/ files/pdf/ Policybrief24.pdf. Accessed 2 March, 2004.

Pelletiere, Stephen C, Editor. *Terrorism: National Security Policy and the Home Front*. Carlisle, Pennsylvania: Strategic Studies Institute, May 15, 1995.

Rice John. *Famous Trials: The Trial of Captain Henry Wirz, Commandant Andersonville Prison, 1865*. The UMKC School of Law Website. [article online] http://www.law. umkc.edu/faculty/projects/ftrials/wirz/wirz.htm. Accessed 2 March, 2004.

Sloan, Frank Keenan. "U. S. Army Role in the Occupation of Japan." Master's Thesis, American University School of International Studies, 17 May, 1965.

Other Resources

Benson, Kevin C. M. Interview By Author. Fort Leavenworth, Kansas. 20 January, 2004.

The Avalon Project at Yale Law School. *The Nuremberg War Crimes Trials*. [website online] http://www.yale.edu/lawweb/avalon/imt/imt.htm#sup. Accessed 10 November, 2003.

Courttv.com. *Transcripts of the Nuremberg Trials*. [website online] http://www.courttv.com/ archive/casefiles/nuremberg/. Accessed 10 November, 2003.

Codification Division, Office of Legal Affairs, United Nations. *United Nations International Law Commission.* [website online] http://www.un.org/law/ilc/introfra.htm. Accessed 14 February, 2004.

International Criminal Trial for Rwanda Internet Task Force. United *Nations International Criminal Tribunal for Rwanda Website.* [website online] http://www.ictr.org/default. htm. Accessed 14 February, 2004.

Internet Unit of the Public Information Services (P.I.S.) of the ICTY. *United Nations International Criminal Tribunal for Yugoslavia Website.* [website online] http://www.un.org/icty/index.html. Accessed 14 February, 2004.

Nationmaster.com. *Demographics of France.* [online] http://www.nationmaster.com/ encyclopedia/Demographics-of-France. Accessed 15 April 2004.

The United Nations International Court of Justice Registry of the Court. *International Court of Justice Website.* [website online] http:// www.icj-cij.org. Accessed 14 February, 2004.

The United Nations Website. [website online] http://www.un.org. Accessed 14 February, 2004,

U.S. Department of State's Bureau of International Information Programs. *Coalition Provisional Authority Website.* [website online] http://www.cpa-iraq.org/. Accessed 4 March, 2004.

Website of the Harry S. Truman Library. [website online] http://www.trumanlibrary.org/ index.html. Accessed 15 March, 2004.

Website of the International Criminal Court. [website online] http://www.icc-cpi.int/ php/show.php?id=home&l=EN. Accessed 19 February 2004.

Website of the 108th Congress, 2nd Session of the United States House of Representatives. [website online] www.house.gov. Accessed 14 February, 2004.

The White House Web Development Team. *The White House Website.* [website online] www.whitehouse.gov. Accessed 14 February, 2004.